A is for

ALMOST ANYTHING

an assortment of poetry

J R Turek

Copyright © 2016 by J R Turek

All rights reserved. No part of this book may be reproduced or transmitted in any form or by any means without written permission of the author.

Cover Art: *Multicolor Futuristic Abstract*
courtesy of *hyena reality* and *FreeDigitalPhotos.net*

Poetry like a box of chocolates…

    you'll never know what you get next.

A is for Almost Anything:

an alphabetic assortment of poetry beginning with the letter A.

No deep, psychological meaning behind the order of the poems, no theme-oriented organization to the sequence, just alphabetic by title.

You never know what the next page will hold so if you dare, my dearest reader, turn the page and read on.

I hope this is the beginning of a unique and wonderful poetic series… I have no fear of getting past Q to X to Z…

Stay tuned for *B is for Betwixt and Between*
and as always,
Write on!

Poetically yours,

~ Judy
    J R Turek

Table of Contents

A Backyard Visit	1
A Bit Jaded	1
A Book With No Cover	2
(a break)	3
A Chance	3
A Christmas Message	4
A Cliché or Two	5
A Day In The Life	6
A Different Perspective	7
a factory for words	8
(a fleck of yellow fur)	8
A Glorious Mystery	9
A Good Book	10
A Great Poem	11
A Headstone, A Little Girl	12
A Holding On	13
A Hyphen Nation	15
(a kiss at midnight)	15
A Knock at the Door	16

Table of Contents

A Lost Soul	17
A Man and A Movie	18
A Man With a Hole in his Heart	19
A Man-Plan	20
A Message from Mother Earth	21
A Moment on Mortality	22
A Mostly Forgotten Friend	23
A New Keyboard	24
A Pile of Random Sweepings	25
A Plain White Envelope	26
(a plane streaks)	27
(a quicksilver sky)	27
(a rabbit in his hat)	27
A Reservoir of Sky	28
A Riddle	29
A Road Away From Here	30
A Scarlet Petticoat	31
(a scarlet urn)	32

Table of Contents

A Second Chance	32
A Secret of Ogres, Trolls, and Earthquakes	33
A Sweet Christmas	34
(a thousand civilizations)	35
(a tow truck towing)	35
(a traveler, summer breeze)	35
A Tree Grows	36
A Virgin Book	37
Aardvark	38
(able to leap tall garden fences)	40
Abigail	40
Abra Cadaver	41
Acceptance	42
Accepted Anonymously	42
Accolades	43
Achilles' Heel	44
Acorn	45
Acoustically Challenged	46
Across the Plains	47

Table of Contents

Addiction on Long Island	48
Advancements	49
Affectionate	51
After All These Years	52
After Dinner Decadence	53
After Hours	54
Agenda: Hunger	55
Aging in Progress	56
Airborne	57
Aliens Have Landed	58
Aliens Land in Merrick	59
All About You	60
All Because of a Parking Space	61
All God's Children	62
All I Never Dreamed Of	63
All My Friends Are Dead	64
All Roads Lead to Christmas	65
Almost Anything	66
Almost Love	68

Table of Contents

Alone	69
Along the Way to Christmas Dinner	70
Alphabetapillar	70
Alteration	71
Alternative Cycle	72
Alternatives	73
Always Blowing	74
Amandacized	75
AMEN	76
America On Wheels	77
American Tapestry	78
Amish Carpenter	80
An American Czech	81
An Apple A Day	82
An Integral Difference	83
An Untold Tale	84
Anatomy of a Nightmare	86
And She's Not Blonde	87
And Suddenly...	88

Table of Contents

And Yet Without It	89
Angels of War	90
Angry Poem	91
Anniversary	92
Anniversary Shopping	93
Annual Maelstrom	94
(another lost earring)	95
(another pen)	95
(another summer)	95
(anything is possible)	96
(aphids invade buds)	96
(apocolipstick)	96
(apples)	96
April	97
Architect	98
Argument	98
Argument Viewed at the Photo Booth	100
Arlington National Cemetery	101
Art of the Bargain	103

Table of Contents

Artistry	104
As Poets	105
Ashes to Ashes	106
At Her Reading	107
At My Demise	108
At the Academy Awards	109
At the Death of Winter	110
At the stroke of midnight	111
At-Home Stress Relief	112
Augmentation	114
August 31, 2008	115
August Days	116
August Eighth	117
Aunt Mary and Uncle Mike	118
Automation	119
Awakening	120
(awkward)	120

A Backyard Visit

She joins me for lunch
Monarch wings of blazing flame
orange, red, yellow
lands upon my waiting hand
flutters fill my hungry heart

(Tanka)

* * * *

A Bit Jaded

Experience
knowledge or skill gained
from personal participation
in living

Experience
speculation clothed in chance
shoed in opportunity
wreathed by risk

Experience
a lesson taught
learned by making
the same mistake twice

Experience
what you get
when you don't get
what you want

A Book With No Cover

Fair warning; I am not what you suppose
pick me up, open me, flatter me
flatten yourself to my pages
allow me, beg and plead, insist that I take you
hold you hostage; let me take your arms
and wrap them around me
      let me see through your brandied eyes
mouth my verse with your painted lips
run your violet-scented hands
through strands of bourbon locks
let them tumble over your shoulder
obscuring a passage of me
then push them away
      let me fill you with desire for more
more, more of my love for you and only you
my quest for the caress of your hands upon my spine
the soft scratch of your bare nail as it fingers
the flesh of my poetry; stop before it's done
emerge with a blank page of your heart
for me and only me
      eyes closed, linger a beat beyond my last line
full of me, yet not sated
never the same
as before you laid eyes on me
before your gaze lingered a moment
then a moment longer at my naked face
until we were locked in a lover's embrace
      a communion of writer and reader
of poet and love
our desires met until we need again
until you read again
don't judge me for what I lack
love me for what I give
more, more, even more the next time

>   a break
>   in the lawn mower song
>   mourning dove

    (Haiku)

* * * * *

A Chance

I cannot take a chance and tell you
How much I love you and need you.

I cannot take a chance and hope you feel the same
For I'd only feel hurt and have me to blame.

I cannot take a chance and love you so much
For how can I be sure there'd be love in your touch?

I cannot take a chance and pretend you love me
I'd only fool the person inside of me.

I cannot take a chance and set you free
There'd be nothing left of life for me.

You're a chance I just cannot take
And a love I cannot forsake.

A Christmas Message
to me

It's Lenox
fine bisque finish
dimensional Mother Mary
cradling Baby Jesus;
at the top, a spun gold braid
ending in a tassel.
Each Christmas,
the ornament lovingly placed
on the face of my tree,
removed after the Epiphany
to cradle in the grey foam contoured box,
the clear plastic sleeve slid back in place
to protect it from exposure to breakage.
Every Christmas since 1991, I think of you –
not with the painful hatred I harbor
eleven months of the year –
but with tender affection for the gift,
the laying aside of differences.
After seventeen years,
destiny directed us to meet
to heal old wounds, to clear a New Year path
clear of animosity. Next week,
when I pack away Christmas, I'll reverence
your ornament, pack it away
with a clear heart, pack it away
for eleven months of hope,
pack it away
as a sacrament of forgiveness.

A Cliché or Two

A challenge
to write
and avoid clichés like the plague
I was all ears, all talk and no action,
and as actions speak louder than words
and being a poet, I had an ace up my sleeve
an ace in the hole and
a whole nine yard-shooting match
all in to win.

What a tangled web we weave
when we lie like rugs, we swim with the sharks
wear concrete shoes,

so I needed to shape up or ship out
I was about to abandon ship
burning the candle at both ends,
burning the midnight oil
long past midnight...

I tried to stay away from them –
absence makes the heart grow fonder
some don't stay away long enough
but they were magnetized to my charms.

Needless to say
this is a cautionary tale
and as luck would have it
I gave it a last ditch effort
and the devil was in the details –
he was dead to rights, a dead ringer for
the elephant in the room.

Plagued by clichés, at the end of the day
I was at the end of my rope
or so it seemed...

A Day In The Life

I wake in warmth of clean sheets,
shower in fragrance of freedom
I, you, we, us chose from a multitude to stuff our hunger,
drive SUVs on streets free of militia, barren of blood stains
to shops, strip malls, grocery stores gorged with more food
in one day than Darfur has seen in years.

She wakes before sunrise to pray, has a cup of tea,
she, Hawa, Khadija, Intisar packs precious possessions,
takes her donkey to the farm, works until the heat
rises beyond bearable, has lunch of berries, works
until the sun sets, goes home.
Meager rations can't feed her large Darfur family;
in their one room house, they go to bed by eight.

I, you, we, us make plans to go out with friends
dinner, a movie, maybe a weekend away to wile away
our unbearable stress; complain about the price of gas,
tuition for our children, sky-high airfares and room rates.

She, Hawa, Khadija, Intisar has never had enough to eat,
searches for water every day, stays home after dark,
keeps her family close, spends time schooling her children best
she can because they have no schoolhouse, no teacher, no books.

I, you, we, us go to the beauty salon for a manicure, pedicure,
hair styled in the latest fashion, outfits closeted by color;
she, Hawa, Khadija, Intisar has nails broken as her spirit,
no shoes, no wardrobe, will not wash her hair for months
for lack of water.

I, you, we, us talk on cell phones, eat fast food,
adjust our thermostats, laze at computers, waste hours
with email, google the Crisis in Darfur;
she, Hawa, Khadija, Intisar has no electric, no refrigerator,
no stove, no spare time of any kind; no hope.

I, you, we, us go to sleep without gunfire for a pillow,
hear planes and helicopters and think of island paradises;
she, Hawa, Khadija, Intisar cowers from planes
with black bellies camouflaged in white bodies
as they drop bombs on her village.

I, you, we, us lock doors on our sumptuous homes
in a faith of safe security; she, Hawa, Khadija, Intisar
is forced from her house to live in an indigent camp,
her husband shot praying for life in a mosque;
she and her children alone in a war zone.

I, you, we, us poets add our voices in awareness
pray for peace in Darfur; she, Hawa, Khadija, Intisar prays
she won't be raped by Janjaweed, prays she'll find firewood
before dusk, prays she'll find water tomorrow,
prays for peace in Darfur.

* * * * *

A Different Perspective

Grieve for the twenty 1st graders
shot dead in Sandy Hook Elementary School...

Grieve for the millions of aborted babies
                    who'll never reach 1st grade...

a factory for words

assembly line workers
pluck twenty-two vowels,
four commas, a handful of dashes
and several scrabble-point letters
at lightning speed from baskets
that hold interchangeable parts
like Barbie's Dreamhouse furnishings
or Uncle Fester's macabre toy chest

they throw the orphan letters
into the mixing vat set to enjamb
and several stanzas down the line
an extruder fills cross-section molds
to just below the syntax line
lets them cure overnight
and next day the next station
binds them into foundling poetry books
sends them to the printer

* * * * *

a fleck of yellow fur
clinging to a cocoon
      butterfly breeze

(Haiku)

A Glorious Mystery
> *for Jeanne-Marie*

a crucifix
a single bead, three beads, a single bead
a medal signifies the first mystery

five decades of ten beads, a single bead
spaced between each, a circle to the medal
linking the trinity beginning and end to eternity

in the beginning, before our bond began
you asked where to go to get a new rosary
I knew then we were destined for more –

without hesitation, opening my purse, giving you
a set of blue crystal beads, ones given me
by a friend and prayed on frequently –

knew without mystery when I passed them on,
they were clasped in good hands, our churchyard hug,
our tears whispered like spoken prayer

and how I told you what was told to me
that when you pray on rosaries, your prayers
touch the person that gifted you those beads

but that was not why I held my hand over yours
the blue beads between us, not begging for your
prayers but knowing they would touch many beyond me

you, returning from The Vatican with a gift for me
lavender crystal beads blessed by The Pope
and you whispering we're both in good hands

on your birthday, when I couldn't be with you
I pulled those lavender beads from my purse
and prayed for you

for us, our beginning to the mystery of eternity

A Good Book

Sinking into a deep cushioned couch
My legs splayed across Paul's lap
Casually crossed at the ankle
His hand lazily massaging my tired feet
His other hand operating the remote control
As he is transported by the television
To a place beyond our living room.
I am transported as well
But my journey is to other places
The picture flashing before my eyes
Are created by my brain waves
Not television waves.
I am immersed in a good book
Living the life
The writer had in mind
For me
Seeing the pictures he's painted
For me
Smelling, hearing, feeling
What he has dictated
For me.
I am comfortable
I am comforted
By the picture we make
My husband and I
Separate, together
Remotely sharing
The peace of following a dream.
I am transfixed by the story
Each word, sentence, page, chapter
It is a good book
Paul is a good man
For me
They were both hard to find
I am lucky to have found them
And to find comfort in both.

A Great Poem

A great poem awakens the sense
To journey through lands of time
And space and infinity
Demolishing thick brick walls
Sharpening awareness; expanding the mind
To quicken the pulse and gently touch
The heart.

A great poem wafts the scent of roses
On a five-fingered breeze
And carries the tang of crabapples
Picked fresh from green trees
Ripped open by pearl-white teeth
Taste buds standing at attention
Imprisoned by soldiers that grind, crush, chew.

A great poem parallels a sable-haired brush
Dripping with light bright blue paint
As it dips and curves and dips
Creating a sky only your mind can see
A brush that dips to dark bright blue
Rising, falling, dipping to an ocean
Clear, cool, translucent.

A great poem sears the skin with heat
Rippling waves of rising, steaming air
That clings and sticks like sweat to flesh
And freezes limbs numb, deadens digits
With howling blasts of cold drafts
Accompanied by drifts of powdery white
To tantalize your senses and make you feel.

A great poem opens eyes to the widest
Hair standing on end, raised gooseflesh
Hammering heart pounding for freedom

Muscles, tensed, tendons coiled, ready

To spring, to soar, to fly beyond sky
Pulse rate heightened, fever burning
Fear losing in the grip of power.

A great poem speaks in a whisper
Deafening in its quietude
Echoes reverberating through the canyons
Between audio sensors, pit-stopping
First at the brain
And landing safely, softly
In the heart.

* * * * *

A Headstone, A Little Girl

A family outing to tend
to weeds, spring plantings
pruned for summer blooms –
places of eternal rest kept neat…

A stone spied an aisle over
when I was five
and she was five less a day
her birthday the same as mine –

that connection
hasn't left me
for a single day
in nearly fifty years.

A Holding On

I would guess I was 7, maybe 8
my brother Mikey 8 or 9 and we were on our way
to spend 8 weeks in Denver, Pennsylvania
but first   we had to stop at the 18th Precinct
Midtown North, Manhattan
my father's 'work' house
so he could arrange to have his paycheck mailed
and to secure his gun

and our mother waited double-parked outside
while the three of us went inside to hails of
Hey Marty! Got yourself two new partners, eh?
Smiles and backclaps and handshakes
and all included us as if we weren't kids anxious
to start celebrating summer. For me, the pool
and the rec hall with the juke box and pinball machines
waiting to swallow my quarters

and for Mikey, the volleyball court and tournaments
and friends held over from last year,
and for my dad, the local yokel accents
and farm foreign slow-down attitude,
and for my mother, shopping in outlet after outlet
and all of it for a whole summer.

It was dark and musty with mile high ceilings,
scuffed tile floors. Perps in cuffs moved by uniforms
from space to place, room to doom, and we scooted
downstairs. More uniformed waves and finally
all the way in the back corner, a matron large as fear itself,
arms folded across an ample chest near bursting seams
on her light blue blouse, her skin a deep raisin brown.
A slow smile spread across her face,
and when she titled her head right, she warmed my heart
with her silent welcome.

Arms unfolded, her crooked index finger,
beckoned Mikey and me forward and we dutifully
followed her command, through a doorway
and she closed the cell door. I clutched Mikey's arm
a sob lodged in my throat cutting off a cry and then
the door flew open. She leaned down –
she smelled like a valley of lilacs –
her smile bright as pearls and asked
You never want to be in there again,
do you? Like attached marionette heads,
we shook them, no-no-no. *Then be good. Always.*

We scampered away from her, past our father
who looked amused yet proud, ran up the stairs
through the corridors and out into the June morning.
Alarmed, our mother opened her passenger door,
worry creasing her brow. Dad lumbered out,
brothers in blue laughing alongside him. He sees
our mother's face, stops laughing, hustles away
from the precinct, gets behind the wheel and we're off
on our way to be swept into summer.

She asks, then demands to know what happened,
why did we look so frightened but he's not saying.
This goes on for nearly a hundred miles until she relents,
relaxes and falls asleep to the somnolent sound
of rubber on macadam. My father spies us in the rearview,
cautions us to never tell

and we won't. Never, not ever saying anything,
not ever going back to that convict green cell
and the barred door with the chipped grey-white paint
and the matron who welcomed our fear
and challenged it to remain with us forever.
To this day, the scent of lilacs makes me sweat.

A Hyphen Nation

   Hyphens are used to join words
separate syllables in a single word,
they are not to be confused with dashes
n and m or en and em or N and M
or a minus sign, which is truly something else.
Hyphens are employed in women's lib
combining his-and-her names, in justif-
ications, in compound modifier constructions.
   There are no spaces before or after a hyphen
except for hanging dangling or floating
hyphens; hyphens are used for repeated words,
and for prefixes and suffixes. Use of hyphens
has been declining in recent years,
our *Shorter Oxford English Dictionary*
dropped 16,000 hyphenated words,
The New York Times sends email not e-mail,
   and now, new & improved words
are becoming two individual words
or one throwntogether word
and so I ask you to please support
the independent state of a Hyphen Nation,
where hyphens can live free
and without fear of extinction.

      *   *   *   *   *

    a kiss at midnight
    another at 12:01
    great way to start the year

(Senryu)

A Knock at the Door

Avon?
Amway?
Not expecting company
house is a mess
Fuller Brush?
Kirby vacuum salesman?
Jehovah Witnesses?
Meter reader?
Census takers?
Bill collector?
FTD Florist?

Oh, Prize Patrol letter said
I may have won five million dollars –
I won! I won!

knock-knock-knock
Toss dirty clothes downstairs
stuff paper piles under couch cushions
throw dishes in dishwasher
I won! I won!

Hurry!
brush hair
lipstick, mascara
evening gown, silver mules
Grandma's diamond earrings
knock-knock-knock

Brush teeth, gargle
chew a dozen TicTacs
spritz Evening in Paris
scrub toilet, wipe sink, Windex mirrors
make bed, pop in Vivaldi CD

knock-knock-knock
woodpecker in oak tree

      (Drabble)

A Lost Soul
    for Anthony

traveling a deserted stretch of nowhere
dust covering shuffling unmetered feet
through brambles of dead branches, leafless limbs
fallen to a hollow shelf of oak shadows

no guides, no signposts, no map
to point the way to civilized society
an outcast on the fringe of wholeness
a misfit among the ostracized at a poetry revival

obtuse angles, not even a square peg
rough cut with splinters spearing
the undone metaphor of starless pillow sky
alone, afraid and lost

in an alley of blackout calendars
hostage to a circuit board of copper wires
mazing through megabytes of false starts
hard stops and abandoned

to a niche in an eave of a forgotten attic
to a musty cardboard seam in a basement box
to a dank trunk in a car-crushing graveyard
hoping, waiting, praying for a patrol

of poetic searchers to rescue it
blow it free of dust, free of confinement
blow it to a southwesterly wind
blow it to a bustling street corner

at the intersection of Lost and Found

A Man and A Movie

New horror flick at the Cineplex;
four phone calls to find a friend to go with;
late for the first show, wait for the second;
hit the concession stand, lounge in the lobby,
roam to the bathroom, come out to find
a hundred people on line. You pay; your date
admits she hates horror but, sigh, will stay anyway.
After a dozen seat changes, after two dozen trailers,
the movie starts. She wants popcorn; no salt, no butter.
Stand in line.
Thirty minutes into blood and gore galore, she requests,
through hands covering her face, a soda. A diet soda
but nothing brown.
You've missed most of the bodies but that's okay. No ice in her
soda; back on line. Now she's off to the bathroom. You slink to
a seat rows away to enjoy the rest of the movie.
With a flashlight carrying usher, she finds you,
hands on hips spitting because these aren't the seats she picked;
they're too close to the screen.
You try the spilled-soda-on-the-seat lie but she's not buying.
You move back three rows, movie-goers complain.
You settle in and it's good; power tools revving, body parts piling
up, and she wants to leave. You convince her the worst is over;
she pouts; you ignore her. And now, arms flailing, popcorn
flying, she's standing in her seat screaming at the screen,
"No! Don't open the door! No! Black-n-Decker Man is there!"
She's sobbing; she's hysterical; she's blonde
and you make a mental note to lose her number.

Movie tickets for two:	$25.00
Refreshments:	$15.00
Taking a chick to a horror movie:	Worthless

A Man With a Hole in his Heart

A man with a hole in his heart
from wanting too deeply, giving
too freely, releasing too little
glued torn pieces of Bukowski poems
over the hole but the man fell in love
again and the hole grew bigger.

Another man with a hole in his heart
lived in a house of cards too long alone,
endless hours shuffling from room
to empty room, solitaire days and nights
with no croupier to keep track
of his losing streak.

A third man with a hole in his heart
from his ball-and-chain tearing away vital
layers like an onion crying insults and rebukes
took her on a cruise, tossed her overboard;
now his heart drowned with her
and there's a hole in his soul.

There's hope for a man
with a hole in his heart, plugged with love,
with want of love, with loss of love
but the man with a hole in his soul
is destined to roam back alleys of hell
forever.

A Man-Plan

If I move this
I'll have to move this other thing first
and then that other, the little shiny one,
will have to go too and it could get lost
or broken, but if I start at the other end
and move that big thing – wait –

I'll have to get help; it's waaaaay too huge
to move myself but if I ask Chuck to help,
he'll want to get paid so forget him. If I ask
Will, he'll bring a case of beer and be toasted
before we start, and if I ask Todd, he'll insist
we get something to eat first,

and we'll end up in McShay's, have bar burgers
and beer, and he'll leave with Cherise or Willow
or whoever happens to be cruising the bar stools
that night and I'll be left alone with the bill, so
not Todd. Yeah, on second thought –
       it's all great where it is, no need to move a thing.

A Message from Mother Earth

Stop.
Think about what you're doing
think about what you're tossing where...
and why.

I am not expendable.
I am not replaceable, nor disposable
but you're pushing me there, propelling
yourselves to an early extinction.

Soon, they'll be no trees to shade beneath
no oak cabinets in your granite kitchen
no maple dresser to hold your silk socks.

They'll be no fish in polluted streams
no white swans on black lakes
not a dewdrop of spring water anywhere.

The air will hack at your lungs, rasp your throat
pepper your skin with welts of inflammation
and that's when you will   Stop

and finally realize
there's no nutritional value in money
and that wealth is not found in a bank vault.

A Moment on Mortality

I pray my words
live on
beyond me
that they settle
in someone's soul
take root, bear fruit
live on
to touch another
generation
and in their germination
spread seeds
to take wing
on prayerful wind.
Lord, let my words sing
long past I am ash
and dust
and let my words touch
the world
if not now
        then when I'm gone.

A Mostly Forgotten Friend

He's gone from our lives many years
we never speak of him, and yet
I suspect that I'm not alone in that
I think of him from time to time.

His presence in our lives served one purpose
he opened the doorway of friendship
for his then-beloved who is now ours
to cherish as only the truest of friends can.

In all the years and all the conversations
we shared as two couples, he made
one profound statement that found a place
deep in my heart and reminds me of you.

With his jaunted chin and cocky smile
that were his and his alone, he said
"Hey Jude, you never, ever
ever do anything small, do you?"

Profound. I learned something
about myself that day. I appreciate
the vastness of his assessment
if not the absence of his presence.

With this knowledge, you understand
why I can never ever ever love you less
than I do, can never ever ever live
with the smallness that was him.

A New Keyboard

So many spaces between words
it's no wonder the spacebar died
collapsed on stilted feet, springs
unsprung, or whatever coerced it
to snap back under my fingertips
with soldiered respect of my authority
each time I ended/started a new
word/sentence/life.

Now this new one beneath my fingers
sharp and preppie, ready to space out
all my thoughts without pounding
but it's different, subtle changes
that cause me pause, like the extra large
delete key where there was just a little guy
and the arrow keys that have no space
between them – I'm south-north-east-westing
all over the page

and do I need a jumbo delete key to eradicate
so many of my words/lines/self, so large
to find it with ease when a stolen couplet
sneaks past and *blast!* it's gone to oblivion
or when my Pulitzer line vanishes
with an errant slip of my right pinkie

and what is that key that's missing
the one below the brooding delete
the little square that could
and I can't remember what it was
or why I need it
but I do.

A Pile of Random Sweepings

\ \ \
/ / /
Patt-
erns
always   patt-
though we   erns
don't see or care
to see them until we need
to build a structure foundation firm
fortress strong a place to nestle inside.
When the world tosses us random
ideas, we need to form them into
order from random piles dropped
at our feet swept into shape brick
building blocks we shift and move
to form a purpose we can live with
live in, live while looking for random patterns always Patterns.

A Plain White Envelope
        from a writing friend

lavender slippers slouch along walkway
directed to red-flag signal
neatly pyramided four-inch stack of dead trees

bills, donation please, bills, bills, bills,
magazines, catalogs, and flyers
all threatened by a gust of wistful wind

cradling contents, lavender slippers shuffle
drop pile on gustless counter
flipping, leafing, tossing near two inches

half-way, hand poised in mid-leaf
hand-addressed with a flourish
half-inch bulging with taped flap
        a plain white envelope

cradling it to my breast, I skip up the steps
sit at my desk admiring the plainness of it
before tearing it open, spilling the contents

such pure delight in pages of mechanical print
bursting with news and updates and anecdotes
dimensional snail mail that is my heart's delight

keep writing, on writing, or not writing
send me the richness, the fullness
the specialness that is you crammed into
        a plain white envelope

a plane streaks
through a summer sky
clouds scatter in its wake

(Haiku)

* * * * *

a quicksilver sky
falls like a magician's cloak
winter dusk descends

(Haiku)

* * * * *

a rabbit in his hat
white fur on his tuxedo
magician's life

(Senryu)

A Reservoir of Sky
The Pine Barrens

Two guides, one ahead, one behind –
a dying cardinal, not yet an adult
lies crying in a sacred forest;
our front leader, Tom, holds him
teaches an impromptu lesson
shows us his fledgling feathers
wing span, raised red crown
head tilted on a weakened neck;
I catch his black bead eye
... and know.

Palm open, he gently places him
on the forest floor,
continues to guide this tour;
I know he does the right thing.
Our back leader, Max, stays behind
cradles the baby in calloused hands
takes him to safety, feeds him
by an eyedropper, slakes his thirst
lets him rest in a nest of newsprint;
he, too, does the right thing.

I am torn – go? follow?
but knowing roots me to the core
standing on the trail, head down
my soul whispering, my mind silent
beneath a reservoir of sky.

A Riddle

It plays with me and I manipulate it
There's never enough
Except when there's too much
Which is rare, very rare.

It appears to expand and contract
Although it's a constant
And never changes
Or does it?

It never ends but it's not a road
Although it can be bumpy
It is neither enemy nor friend
But can be made to be both.

It heals all but is not a doctor
It lessens grief but never mourns
It tells all but never speaks
It reduces mountains to dust without a sound.

It creates memories
Without blinking an eye
It is a sponge that soaks up
And never gives back what it has taken.

It cannot be created
But is often squandered
It cannot be patented
But oh if it could I'd be a millionaire!

My favorite enemy
               .....time.....

A Road Away From Here

On a road away from here, she crooks
her index finger like a question mark
beckons me to denounce my visit
to a sick friend, instead to spend some time
at the five-and-dime, matinee the day away
at the Main Street Playhouse.

The road is dressed in cinnamon
with a rank undercoat of decay,
her laugh mimics a rasp cackle;
I cough to clear the air I inhale
clear my head of the morse code
of warnings that erupt at her calling.

The road is not a road at all
but a free-fall roller coaster with no cars,
no tracks, no calliope to cover moanings
creeping up from below; fear crawls
on my flesh, soaks my collar in sinister
streams of sweat, shivers me in dread.

Her skeleton hand clamps an icy grip
I shake her off my shoulder,
eyes forward
focused on my destination
the road that leads back
back to the safety of you.

A Scarlet Petticoat

My guess is that Saint Patrick and Brigid of Kildare
were shooting the Irish breeze one fair 5th century day
and decided to give women a break. *Wouldn't it be grand
for a lass to propose marriage? Sure-n-be-gora,
it'd have to be a fine day, an exceptionally special day,*
and so it was that Leap Day, February 29th every four years
(with mathematic exceptions) would traditionally be the day of
women's right to propose.

I can guess that this was tough, that tears could last four years
until leap year again, that broken hearts swam in emerald seas of
misery, that something had to be done.
Queen Margaret of Scotland (who was age 5 and living
in Norway at the time) signed a law that required fines be paid if
a proposal was refused. The groom-not-to-be would be levied
anything from a kiss to a silk dress.

I'm guessing this didn't go over well with menfolk;
pitching woo became more a game than fair play;
and so, to even the score a might,
women were to wear a scarlet petticoat as a warning.
Leap Day has bloomered once again so fess up, lasses;
draw up your dresses and reveal your red intentions.
And in the interest of fair,
skirt out the back, guys; run, run!

>   a scarlet urn
>   collecting June dewdrops
>   blossoming rose

(Haiku)

* * * * *

A Second Chance
    for Adam

A chance encounter
I've converted, he says
I'm Catholic now
a new chapter in a new book,
a second chance.
Please,
anything I've done
everything I've done to offend you,
berating abuse to make you hate me,
please –
I stop his flow of raw thorns
on my hatred of him harbored so long,
bestow on him a hug longer than a breath,
longer than the seconds it takes to forgive
seventeen years of festering his memory
in a maggot-filled corner of my heart.
In the release of our embrace,
a purging, a purity,
a second chance at redemption.

A Secret of Ogres, Trolls, and Earthquakes

pins and needles ransom me to sleep
stabbing me to nightmare restraints
fairytales of ogres ransacking chain-mail castles
iron-studded whipcracks emblazon tattoos
on my bare biceps held firm by gnarled hands
bog green flesh rippling with pulse points of ebony blood
encrusted across hairy knuckles creaking with effort,
an ogre invades my sleep, rips lavender dreams from my head
steals peace, beats me deeper into his nightmareland,
why me? but there's no answer; his roar demands silence,
whipcrack falls to oaken floor and rattles the earth
silent screams waltz my flailing legs, calypsoing through
swampy sheets dripping with rotted flesh of bleeding salmon
pink and red and black pooling under me, floating me off
to mistful forest of dead trees petrified by trolls
that weep acid drops on sullen growth, decorating the land-
scape with dread and despair, searing tarantula flesh
with dripping purple saliva, sucking juice from swollen bodies
as from a ripened orange, pale concrete troll-flesh
turning persimmon when sated, he siestas under canopies
of frozen fingers pointing to redemption
why me? I scream, a silent echo returns no answer
troll-snores shake the moon from star-studded foundation
it splits in two falling with a shimmering wake upon a troll
in the dead forest and upon the head of my chartreuse ogre
outside prince harming's castle, they charge, rumble over
owning me, explosions thunder over mountain ranges, stomping
upon satin sheets of sod, my ogre yanks at ground crust, cleaving
mountain fissures, christened greedy earth-mouth swallows,
raging troll spitting fire spears as he descends to earth's gullet
engulfing ogre in waves of grave soil, blanketing their shrieks
to eternal damnation, sod rolling over mountaintops valleys,
plains and forests waking to a new moonless day
I escape to bruised wakefulness
too once-upon-a-time to stay asleep

A Sweet Christmas

On the first day of Christmas, my true love gave to me
a pound of Belgian chocolates. On the second day,
he gifted me with a pound of dark chocolate truffles
and another 16 ounces of Belgian chocolates.

On the third, fourth, and fifth day,
he presented me with Godiva, Ghiardelli, and Lindt
and another serving of the aforementioned.

On the sixth, seventh, and eighth day, he introduced me
to MarieBelle, Romanico's, and Payard's chocolates,
along with yet another helping of all that came before.

On the ninth, tenth, and eleventh day, he bestowed upon me
ganache, praline, and hazelnut, and you guessed it,
more of the riches past.

On the twelfth day, he granted me a pound
of dark chocolate covered cherries in Chambord cream
and a repeat of the previous eleven days.

So when you get your Christmas card this year
decorated with chocolate smudges, you'll know
I'm indulging in the 364 pounds of decadence
my true love gave to me for Christmas this year.

a thousand civilizations
under one roof
library

(Haiku)

* * * * *

a tow truck towing
a tow truck –
traffic stops to watch

(Senryu)

* * * * *

a traveler, summer breeze
blows us closer and closer
to autumn

(Haiku)

A Tree Grows

Center of a woman's closet floor
a shoe tree branches out –
at the root base, spikes, hikers
and rainbow-hued sneakers
lower limbs suspend ballerina flats
moccasins, oxfords, and lazy loafers
a trunk of 9-to-5 conservative heels
ringed by pumps in calf-leather
fabric, patent, and suede.

The tree grows by season sales –
balance perfect platforms and wedges
sheltered by slingbacks and ankle straps
dazzled over by canopies of clogs,
peep toes and strippy stilettos
a forest of fur-capped mules and booties
beaded slides and jeweled thongs
a crown of trendy t-straps in metallic
velvet, satin, and lucite.

Listen for the gasp as the door opens
the whispered pleas of *pick me pick me*
pairs flashing buckles, tapping toes,
showing off the perfect match for your outfit
all waiting to leave the shoe tree
for a healing outing, a brisk striding,
a stretching stroll to the mall –
all longing for the caress
of an instep.

A Virgin Book

Blank pages beckon to be satiated
splayed with ink, splattered with words
filled to spilling, like your old journal
that gluttons open on your desk
bulges from three sides and won't stay shut.

This new book, each page a waiting sponge
for jottings and mind meanderings
and even that quick reminder
to pick up the dry cleaning.

Glue bound, glossy bright
white pure paper
you're assured is acid-free
to retain your words for centuries.

You bought two, a red and a blue
high hopes of writing often
to be prepared when your muse appears
and demands to be heard.

You finger the bold cardinal cover,
pleather that holds up better than hide
in unpredictable weather;
you'll carry it everywhere.

There
the first page, first spot of ink
your name and today's date
... a great beginning.

Aardvark

Spring has sprung and once again
we have ants – on kitchen counters,
in the sink, little black ants in the bathroom,
colonists scampering across white tile
showering with me,
easy enough to swish down the drain
but why are they here
and how do we get rid of them?

Last year, we put traps everywhere,
after several weeks, no sightings
but it was late summer, autumn falling in...
did they move to a temperate climate,
vacationing abroad through winter?
Though I can't blame them, it seems
our address is an ant retreat hotspot.

While watering my Hawaiian orchids
a troupe of a hundred of them
marched out of the soil, down the side
of the white ceramic heart pot,
disappearing under the window moulding.
Bugaphobic, my brain screamed
Do something!

I googled 'ant removal' and found

Aardvark: Afrikaans for 'earth pig'
though not related to the pig;
nocturnal ant and termite eater;
4 toes on front feet, 5 on rear feet
each toe has a flat shovelesque nail,
part claw, part hoof; weigh about 150 lbs,
up to 7 feet long, tail included.

*Teeth have no enamel coating,
are worn away, regrow continuously;
long sticky tongue extracts insects
from underground mounds.
Sole extant representative
of the mammalian order Tubulidentata,
fossils dated to 5 million years.*

So sad, the sole survivor!

*Large upstanding ears for keen hearing
helps protect from predators,
long snout for supersonic scenting
allows aardvark to find food
traveling as many as 19 miles in a night,
can dig a yard of tunnel in 5 minutes,
can live up to 23 years in captivity,*

... can find and eat 50,000 insects per night.

He'd only go out at night, he's a bit furry
and would blend in with our dogs...
he's quite a digger, we could plant the garden
in record time, and if the termites come back...
but I wonder, do you need a license
to own an aardvark?

         able to leap tall garden fences
         the squirrel
         eats my tomatoes

(Haiku)

* * * * *

Abigail

I saw it swinging in the Salem breeze
a noose of hemp woven by a neighbor
kin perhaps, a noose knotted to fit my neck.

I saw it waving above the pine platform
where my black button-ups would soon swing
beneath my tired black skirt.

The trial, more mockery than democracy.
Sentenced to hang til my neck snaps
and death snatches me.

Their fear is a taste I savor.
Standing on that platform, I'll curse them,
their offspring for a hundred generations.

My neck in that noose,
smoke curls from my tongue to their hearts.
Never mess with a witch.

(Drabble)

Abra Cadaver

mesmerized by the sign outside
I linger on the threshold of a small
nondescript storefront
    tucked in a row of For Rent signs
    in a secluded part of town
    a ghastly screech tapers from the jamb
as I enter the mysterious dark cavern
where a cumulus of smoke signals
spiral over firebowls of scented wax
    wicks of hypnotizing flames
    surrounded by color-changing lakes
    of molten lava in cauldron-hot glass jars
a ceiling fan center of the shop
swirls the smoke like gauze strips
lit by a harvest moon globe of light
    the shop is coffin quiet, gloomy
    as the early October darkness
    peering through the glass door
I browse table to table sniffing
pumpkin spice, crisp candy apples
cinnamon, jasmine, and something
    that tugs at a buried memory...
    I rake in a carnival of sealed jars
    take them to the register
but no shopkeeper greets me
a loan moan rises through the scarred
oak floor, goosebumps riddle my limbs
    blood freezes in my veins
    I can't breathe, can't scream
    as a phantom hand grabs my shoulder
I turn, stare into emptiness dense
as cemetery fog, leave my purchases
fleeing to the safety of the acorn-littered street

Acceptance

You are moving on
to acceptance.

Accept the love and friendship
from those worthy of giving it
and receiving it.

Accept the fact that you cannot cure all ails
nor can you fix the unredeemable.

Accept that you are in charge of your emotions.
Smile when it hurts the most and you'll still
be smiling when the pain passes.

* * * * *

Accepted Anonymously

I finally realized
the problem.
I don't drink alcohol.
I drink distilled spirits.
Therefore,
I accept that I am not
an alcoholic.
I am purely
spiritualistic.

Accolades

We clap
for joy, for praise, for others;
we clap
at the close of movies,
at stock car races,
at poetry readings.
We clap
when the applause sign lights up,
when first-graders perform a play,
when our star athlete scores a point,
a goal, a home run, a touchdown.
We clap to express happiness,
to honor a speaker, to fan a rock group
for an encore, to encourage a comedian
to keep on keeping us laughing.
We clap, fingers tingling, standing ovations
for an artist dipping his brush, his pen,
into elation to radiate to waiting hearts,
gratitude for a gift given, a gift received.
Sometimes
we clap
because it's over.

Achilles' Heel

That soft, tender spot
Achilles' mother left unsubmerged on his heel,
his weak point left vulnerable for Paris' arrow –
that soft, tender spot
not on my heel but slithering up to undiscipline me
weaken me in submissive adulation –
      men/young, guys/old – it doesn't matter –
      long locks flowing over broad shoulders
      lengthy neat, clean, cared-for male hair
      reconditions me, pulse races, pupils dilate
      to leave me head over hair infatuated.
Last week while window shopping on a city street
      I saw auburn waves tied up in a nylon rubberband
      above a three-piece pinstripe
      a lust tingled behind my knees for an hour;
      and out with a man-friend to a sports arena,
      permed, loose ringlets wrestling in skin tights
      had me slut-swooning ringside,
      had my crew-cut companion seething green;
      on a nature tour, trudging wooded trail, two steps ahead,
      stick straight raven braid down the center of a back
      packed with ripples bulls-eyed quivers up my spine.
Everywhere I am, male tresses curling out to me
      beseeching me to run palms through manes, tuck stray
      angel wisps on bare necks back into banded confines,
      combined with clean-shaven face, I'm helpless, senseless,
      head over achilles' in love.
      Uncontrolled gasping grunts in reply to *Hi,* I subway
      straphang, hold on for breath, it's dark and kinky
      drawn up in a rawhide tie beneath a chestnut cowboy hat,
      and I want to ride him unbridled all the way to Texas.
Today, visored sun-bronzed highlight blonde lifeguards me
as I sink in waves begging to be saved
but there's no hope for me
no cure for that soft spot
not on my heel but slithering   so   far   higher.

Acorn

With cap and coat, an oak tree's legacy
falls heavily to mother earth
stays close to mother tree;

these progeny scooped up by squirrels
cached in knotholes or buried
to stave off a starving winter.

Others consumed by deer in autumn
or beaked up by bluejays
hoarded for frost warnings.

A staple high in protein, fat, carbs
acorns are tender, succumb
to mold, especially if hidden

beneath fallen layers of leaves;
these seeds cease to be
a new generation of oak trees.

These warriors stand for enduring patience;
oaks live two hundred plus years
produce thousands of acorns annually.

Gatherers drop stray acorns
to land far from momma
to germinate, sprout roots,

shoot forth a sapling,
growing, maturing, becoming
in twenty-five years, a mother tree.

Acoustically Challenged

It's possible he's lost his hearing
hard to say if he's deaf
so I employ patience, repeat things
twice and wait for a response,
a reaction, something.

When I get nothing, the third time
becomes a shout. Lo and behold,
a miracle occurs – his cochlea,
eustachian tube, and stirrup work;
his hammer hits anvil onto
his tympanic membrane,
his eardrum reverberates sound
and glory be, he can hear.

Perhaps he thinks I suffer from
a similar affliction because he yells
I heard you the first time!
I whisper a suggestion that, in the future
he respond even with a grunt
so I know he heard me.
In a lower whisper, I suggest a visit
to an audiologist, a light comment
that hearing aids these days are small,
nearly undetectable, and a second shout
I'm not deaf!

And I wonder if that's true and perhaps
there's a switch he controls
for selective hearing.

Across the Plains
   for Maxwell Corydon Wheat, Jr (3/18/1927-6/7/2016)

A pheasant squawks my attention
waves wood-tone fringe of feathers
fanned eastward in early mating season;
he touches down on the far side of road adjacent
to the Hempstead Plains; a glossy white SUV
stops at the octagonal red sign for his passing,
a sign of respect that his ancestors graced this plain
long before man-made motors, long before caterpillar
was connected with dirt moving, foundation pouring,
commerce infringing on nature, long before
the Hempstead Plains yielded a sign of passage.

Beside a yellow road sign, his mate waits
smaller, less adorned, yet regal with head held high
as her mate cries her name, heralds her
behind the screen of bushes
on the verge of the Hempstead Plains,
witness to the future of handmaid moths,
bushy rock rose, wild indigo, green milkweed
a sanctuary of grasshopper sparrows,
sandplain gerardia, and fields of bird's foot violets
striving to survive across the screen,
across the road, across the plains of history.

Addiction on Long Island

She's doling out poetry prompts
at the water cooler, in the lobby of a trendy restaurant,
in the ladies rooms; she thinks of herself as a drug porter
delivering a fix of alliteration to syntax starved poets
closeted in Boise, the Ozarks, and Mayberry. She refuses
to surrender to complications like planning, shopping, cooking
for family-night dinner when there's poetry to ingest.

Her pupils are dilated, she's wired tight
and wasting no time flipping out poetry flyers
to everyone on trains, buses, and street corners
like there's a national emergency with no free-time
to waste on laundry, or pressing corsages of metaphors
on a teflon-covered ironing board, no spare seconds
to check traffic, to pack, no less to rummage the Louis Vuitton
luggage from the hall closet. The world needs to know–
there are poetry events nearly every night!

In her desperation to avoid weddings and christenings,
graduations and birthday parties, she tries lying
that it's not about poetry, not about her need
but the similes catch in her throat and she relents
to sit at a back table, scrawling assonance-rich lines
on linen napkins she'll stuff in her baggage-big purse.

Forgive her, she's addicted to poetry; megapixel inspirations
revolve in her head like the carousel at the Farmer's Market,
white stallion rondeaus calliope with pantoums and sestinas
until she's about to burst with needing a keyboard, a pen
and journal, or her greatest fear will befall –
abandoning an infant poem to the pain of never being
and so she lives poetry, shares it, spreads it
like grape jelly on whole wheat toast –
poetry: her drug, her addiction.

Advancements

Picture this:
two old biddies
sitting behind bullet-proof glass
counting their till of stolen souls,
one eye panning the streets
for a waif in need of food and water
but she'll find no salvation
from these two relics
who remember the dawn
of time, watched earth unfold
into day and night,
fought to keep their place
above the flames,
trickeries and deception
have kept them here
for centuries.

In this incarnation,
these demons are pawn brokers
trading meager pennies
for anything worth stealing
to anyone worth cheating.
They breathe easy
inside their ballistic-proof
room with a view
from gangsters carrying
firepower bursts
bled by just a breath
on a hair trigger,
bloodied souls fresh,
not yet resurrected
from maggot-mouthed graves
though their day will come
to join living-dead souls
(like those of the biddies

*taking their smoking guns
giving them new ones to play with)*

*and the ganglanders collect their weapons,
heft them like babies born to crack addicts
and heroine fiends, use them as shields
against bigger guns
carrying deadlier rounds.*

*They notch their clubs with each kill,
glory in the gory
and praise technological advancement
of artillery from puny .22s
to hand cannons meant to annihilate,
these hoodlums trade up
their old machine guns to warfare gunmetal
that glints in blood day sun
strapped on their shoulder
like the latest Gucci bag.*

*The soul of that poor waif
is safer with the ganglanders
than those two wicked witches
who won't stop torturing
when the heart stops pumping,
their need to maim
is greater than the gangs,
these barren beasts,
these hematite-hearted warriors
with their empty eyes
have survived every evil act conceived
but even their transparent armor
can't hide
their need to shatter anything
they can't control.*

Affectionate

I found it hanging around
my backyard, a stray,
scruffy, in need of a bath
quiet, well-behaved,
grateful.
It was just me
so cooking a little extra
was no problem.

It was a he.
He'd sit beside me
on the patio bench
licking my hand
long after he'd eaten
the steak or chicken
I hand-fed him.
Those soulful eyes –
I soon welcomed him inside.

That's when I realized why
he was a stray.
Hogging the couch,
belching, farting,
demanding I get him
a beer. I threw him out.
Told him to go back to his wife.
That poor, poor woman.

(Drabble)

After All These Years

Though I find fault
I love you
though you chew a little loud
and compete with the tv volume
kept so low, I've learned
to read lips

though you snore
and talk in your sleep, argue
with me at 3 in the morning
that you're awake and it's the dog
who snores

though you procrastinate –
confession, so do I
and though we've been together
so long, we finish each other's thoughts
we complete each other

and though you may think I complain
I love you more each magical moment.

After Dinner Decadence

crystal moments string together
like faceted beads on filament-thin
minutes
waiting, watching, sighing
for the first sign, an initial bubble
to break the surface of semi-sweet serenity

sturdy stoneware bowls circle
in anticipation, embracing delicate
ladyfingers
luscious berries, stemmed cherries
fresh pineapple wedges
and crystalized ginger chunks

crispy-thin potato chips, biscotti,
mystical pretzels knotted with patience
languish
on winter white platters
with long-handled forks
beside a cerulean sterno flame

tonight, a dash of Bailey's
next week, a jigger of Grand Marnier
decadence
in decadence, in smooth spooned swirls
steam ascending in heart-shapes
– it's ready for dipping

it's February 14th today,
and every Saturday, it's
Valentine's Season –
what better reason to fondue
a blustery night
in chocolate smudged kisses

After Hours

Sun rays slant through
hand hewn glass panes
of the old hat shop;
a lock click signals the start
of a moonlit serenade.
A black top hat and a rose-covered cloche
waltz across the gleaming wood plank floor
a purple-veiled pillbox and a tan ten-gallon cowboy
two-step to twanging chords only they can hear
a forest beret and a sapphire ostrich toque
circle around brown derby and picture perfect onlookers
beyond sombreros and trilbies, fedoras and straw leghorns
tapping time with bonnets brimming with ribbons
tricorns, homburgs, and black velvet opera hats
spin on their racks
boaters and sailors sway in place
tall, elegant hat pins stand en pointe
till a lock click signals the end
of the last dance
until closing time

Agenda: Hunger

hunger rumbles through empty alleys
cries out for something fulfilling
crashes to the depth of depression
falls without a ladder or hand up
no hand-outs with hunger

hunger devours hope, lashes out
at those least able to defend themselves
hunger stalks the strong, kicks their feet
out from under them
hunger unbalances everything

hunger demeans the proud
destroys the faith in self-sustaining
endures all evils for the sake of withholding
threatens to change a positive outlook
to a permanent sadness

hunger doesn't discriminate
doesn't ask your name
doesn't care your age, your IQ
your political stance, race creed
or whether you had a happy childhood

hunger doesn't relent for seniors   or the disabled,
will not STOP   for kids
who have no voice, no access to adult programs,
kids who go to school hungry because
they had no dinner and breakfast is a mirage
on a far-off galaxy, lunch spent hiding out
to avoid detection   explanation   pity,
kids who suffer through class, brain cells dying
for a hot meal, good nutrition, something to make
the growling in their stomach and their head stop

hunger doesn't care   hunger maims

hunger   left hungry   kills

Aging in Progress

Sitting at your kitchen table
years ago/months ago/seems like yesterday
I roll my eyes, tap my feet, sigh
at yet another tale retold verbatim
wondering how you could forget
you've recited this childhood recollection
a dozen times, performed with the same
hand motions and voice inflections,
how could you go on and on story after story
how you could miss my reaction
(or did you?).

Standing before your alabaster stone
I learn to love what I long to see
berate myself for not paying attention
not listening to the gift of your treasures
not jotting down your beloved memories
which can never be mine
as they have slipped from me
like you –
tears trace empty lines on my cheeks
as I press palms to my ears
to shut out the gnawing, prying silence.

Kneeling today at your resting place
my incessant chatter fills the silent void
I plant smiling-faced chrysanthemums
bursting with sun-yellow buds
bare hands pat the sacred soil that holds you
attentive to my grief
water lavishly
vow to come back tomorrow, the next, verbatim –
pay attention to blossoms aging in progress
in reverent memory
of you.

Airborne

Germs travel in crowded company
infest schoolrooms, shops, and libraries
tap shoulders with a host, infiltrate
innocent sinus, lungs, throat.

Though I occasionally catch a cold
that's not the source of my rantical diatribe –
it's those calorie germs that afflict me, stick
to my hips as my starved stomach rails
against germs of apple pie, chunks of dark fudge
brownie, high-fat ice cream in any flavor.

They're cunning, these calorie germs
never adhering to lettuce leaves or carrot
sticks, never hibernating in low-sodium
soup, never propagating in yogurt (except
the frozen kind, and only if it's not vanilla)
never ever multiplying in water –

yet that's what I consume and I know
they're not there (the FDA says so) –
it's not fair, I tell you, the gurgling
you hear is my hunger; I should be
a size three but no, it's their sadistic plan.

Now I'm on to their tricks as they ingest treats –
they eat, you eat, everyone eats, but me. Mega-
chunk chocolate chip cookies, mousse with whipped
cream cheese icing on a stick, streusel strudels
swimming in cane syrup – they're infested with them

and these calorie germs jump from your plate
and take flight
right   to   my   thighs.

Aliens Have Landed

    I see them at night, on our bed –
hovercrafts like blue marbles exploding
with white centers that crackle with a single
high-pitched note before they're crushed.
    Oddly, they're attracted to Ruffles –
when he stretches, searches for a more comfortable
position on the bed, turning in circles,
not three times as most dogs do,
but in nine circles before curling up.
    It's in those nine circles I see the invaders
float below his massive paws, disappear
then rise with each prancing step, like a comet tail
that flashes before extinguishing.
    I wonder how long they've been here
how many nights I'm tucked up, tuckered out
not watching at 3am when they appear,
and what do they want with us, what plan
what purpose, what will they make us do,
what will they do to us, what have they done,
    and I wonder why it's only Ruffles, our largest –
most intimidating in size, most skittish disposition
that they are drawn to. And why, oh why
isn't Ruffles frightened?
    Last night, hand shaking with trepidation
I reached out to Ruffles, blue lights blinking
on off beneath his feet, his fur still as soft
as a puppy, and I yank my hand back.
    Shocking explosion of brilliant blue light
bit my hand. Pain tingles for a moment
fades with the blue haze.
    Ah.
Soft afghan
soft fur
air electrically charged –
    well, I thought they were aliens.

Aliens Land in Merrick

Daylight grellow eyes flash unseen
(my eyes closed on their arrival)
their ship a crash site alongside
raised railroad tracks
they infiltrate Long Island, waltz down
Sunrise Highway, scan strip malls
stripped of a prosperous economy
and impressed by their reflection
in polarized panes, they enter the edifice
where I wait, ride the glass elevator up
stroll down hallways till they find me
hovered in a tunnel that seemed so wide
until they slid me in, warned not to move
(if you do, you'll have to endure the MRI
all over).

Intrigued, they slide inside the metal tube
rattle rivets, crash around like astronauts
in a zero gravity universe. These aliens
my test companions, sing, hum, play drums
they recite poetry to me, though headphones
try to hide their rantings, incessant bangings
their impish wailings to go home.
After remaining statue-still for a half-hour
I am released from my mid-town tunnel
confinement; fear abated, I thank the aliens
wish them well and they cry like infants
that I'm going home
and they're not.

All About You

The *u* in us slants in italics
a better view for you to gorge
on your reflection in silvered glass,
revel in the world-wide arrogance
that is not us, but you, all you,
and nothing but you.

The *s* in us appears in phonetic type
a size 4 font barely visible beside you,
a tiny squiggle nearly non-existent
beside the pomposity of you –
the s is me and may as well be
a stray mark on your page.

The you in us is magnified 200%
for headline reading from across
a street crowded with gapers
ogling the bold face you publish,
underscoring there's no you in sharing;
one for you and all for you.

There is no more me in us, no we,
no compromise for us,
just you, you,
y
o
u-u-u.

All Because of a Parking Space

Near impossible to park in Manhattan
especially on a summer Sunday afternoon
but we're young and rebellious, circle the block
several times before a car pulls out just behind us.

Paul gushes *Get out, hold the space, just stand there
I'll drive around the block. Go, go I'll be right back!*

I'm not a big fan of The City and we're going to visit
his mother so my mood was perhaps not jubilant.
I defend the space, cars honking at me
but I'm determined to stand my ground until an SUV
pulls in, inching so close I flinch from the radiator heat.

It was an act of self-defense – I backed up
he inched forward, I backed into the car behind me.
I was pissed that I'd lost round one but not ready to give up.
He sneered a snide remark at me, chirped his alarm,
puffed out his chest, arms curled at his side
and strutted across the street.
Something in my demeanor must have signaled
a wariness as he turned around, swiping peeks
over his shoulder before he turned off 70th onto York.

I lit a cigarette, hands shaking with frustration
and yeah, maybe just a chink of fear, and I bent
toward his 17" high-end Michelins mounted
on deep-dish chrome Cragars and sucked my cig
to blazing red, turned it between thumb and index
pointed the lit end to the front tire...
though I wouldn't have done anything.

It didn't take long before he was cursing back
to his truck, alarm chirp on off on off, doors locked,
he cursed some more fist waving fury, got in, sped off
leaving some of those Michelins behind.

In motion-picture timing, Paul turns the corner
pulls in to the space, gets out laughing
See that wasn't so bad...
        It was a very quiet Sunday afternoon.

All God's Children

I dreamt I was an angel
Sent from up above
To send to each of you
Some special words of love.

I dreamt I was angel
A postman from the sky
To say "You must use your wings
If you ever expect to fly."

I dreamt I was an angel
With some advice to heed today
Remember, the beginning of your life
Begins again each day.

I dreamt I was an angel
To send a message to you
God created life for you
So put life in all you do.

All I Never Dreamed Of

My poetry always lies
big bass concocted tall tales of inaccuracy
bearing false witness, exaggerating bluefish stories
fibbing, floundering, fable myths sprawled
like chicken cutlets in the bareboard seafood bins
of downtown dim-lit streets.

No fluke, no coincidence that my poetry falsifies
testifies through forked-tongue dinners of defamation
deceiving, misleading, perjured whoppers
of misrepresentation. What you must think of me
as my poetry stretches along, spreads along,
slanders along an alley of fiction, painting me Picasso
with distortions, plastic gems glued as subterfuge
over lidless eyes large as pizza pies
stocked with salmon, sardines, and anchovies.

Stanzas stray, perched to once upon a double-dealing,
underhanded, contrived disguised time of lies.
Libel lines angled through fakery, my poetry lies –
except when the truth will do to subdue
the desire to fabricate, when cod bob
in my fish tank, when casting integrity is sincerity
when righteous wins and lecherous loses,
when treacherous treads an angelfish path;
that when is all I never dreamed of.

Disreputable red herring, dishonorable carp,
double-crossing disloyal trumped-up trout –
my poetry lies, you see; hooked, I'm the bait
caught in a trawler's net; honest,
it's not me that lies;
it's my poetry.

All My Friends Are Dead

      She says this to me as though
I asked her; I don't know her.
"I've outlived them," she says, knuckles
jutting from arthritic fingers that clutch
the dull aluminum frame of her walker.
      "All my friends are dead," she repeats
leaning closer to me as though I were
hearing impaired.
To keep her from leaning any closer
I raise eyebrows in line with my "Oh."
She settles back on the heels of her clunky
black orthopedics.
      Deep in thought, her hands spasm in time
with her tongue licking lips already moist
with spittle, a tiny ribbon of which rolls
down her chin, catches on a stray grey whisker
caught like prey in a spider web.
I try not to stare.
      "Marge was the last. She made it to 92
but after she broke her hip, it broke her heart
and her spirit. We buried her last month."
Head tilting to the right, I express my sympathy,
not daring to ask how old she is to have outlasted
all her friends.
      Like a finger of intuition, she sighs into a chuckle,
shifts her weight to the left and says "I'm 94,
stuck here in the old fart home all alone."
She inhales so deeply that she sways, I reach out
to steady her but she glares.
      "I've outlived all my enemies, too."
I pull my hand back. "I am here forever,
here to pass judgment on the young, here to accuse
the guilty, here to keep everyone in line, follow my
rules or leave. I'm here forever so I must be doing
something right.
      Did I tell you all my friends are dead?"

All Roads Lead to Christmas

Christmas will pass me by on the Holiday Highway
creeping along the shoulder of Procrastination Blvd;
refusing to turn off to Belated Lane, I race my engines
with 7-11 high-test pedal to the metal to the mall
zigzagging a thoroughfare of dazed shoppers
trailing from boutiques to department stores,
stalling at kiosks along the route.

I'm determined not to cross the finish line last
topping my cart with listed gifts, bopping crossroads
of aisles aKringle with seasonal greetings, shopping
Candy Cane Lanes ablaze in twinkling lights,
stopping at Saint Anthony's, dropping to knees
before the manger, follow the path of prayer
to make this Christmas the best ever.

Expressway traffic is a viaduct of red lights
blinking on and off, turn off to a turnpike
of green lights for miles, smiles as late shoppers
breeze the byways to get just one more gift
before the stores close on Christmas Eve. Blazing star
guides me home to wrap, carols playing, my heart ajingle
with a Christmas tingle of finishing on time.

Almost Anything

Always be prepared
like a girl scout, or a cub scout –
I was both, honorary cub because my brother
was in the troop, our mother was scout leader,
I didn't like my Monday after-class dance lessons
and I was ready for anything,
though I never got to enter my whittled car
in the soapbox derby
and that's ok because I liked the guy stuff
better than sewing and baking
yet I can crochet you a blanket of wishing.

Almost anything can manifest
when you least expect to see your breath levitate
on a cold cloud, feel sweat pool in the crook
of your elbow, awaken at 3am to find your heart
racing like an Indy 500 winner and the house
cemetery stone silent
and the quiet reminds you that everything
is ok.

Anything can ensue when you flip open
the box cover and see what waits inside –
caramel, pecan cluster, butter truffle
vanilla ganache, dark chocolate cashew chews
nougats with your dentist's name engraved in them.
Sweet anticipation, decadent intoxication
a dark chocolate reason to live
and that's ok with me.

Anything can appear when you flip open
the book and see what waits inside
enticed by a vibrant cover promising
an engaging vacation away from your life
chaptered with excitement and intrigue
a deep mysterious reason to read
and that's ok, too.

Anything can call to you from the next page
whisper your name in coconut cream seduction
strum your heart tune from strings connected
to your poetry soul, tap your toe to melancholy blues
and it's all good, it's all ok.

Anything can threaten to steal your happiness
rock your boat, reach up, drag you down a black abyss
and it's easy to forget that you are in charge
of how you feel, how you react, how you let go
of the bad and grasp the good for all it's worth

and soon you see life isn't all
the dark-chocolate-covered raspberry creams
everyone hopes for
and that's really ok, too.

Almost Love

She giggles shyly and looks up over her book
quickly his eyes dart back to his paper
all around are signs of spring and new life
above the birds chirp love songs to the flowers.

Slowly she peeks over the binding and once again
their eyes meet for a split second
quickly they escape back to their printed words.

Beginning as a light drop here and there
a spring storm pops up with little warning
each one hustles quickly out of the rain
cursing the shower and the ill-timed intrusion
regretting their shyness
they part strangers, having never met.

Fate has deemed
they will never meet again.

Alone

God, I try to forgive you the small act
of selfishness when you waved your Almighty hand
the unannounced invader, the unwelcome visit
when your spirit did not rise alone.

God, I want to forgive you this injustice, this theft
in the death of night without warning, this darkness
that has invaded me, chilled my faith in you, you've
stolen from me and I'm left alone.

God, I beg you, help me –
how can I go on without my first dance partner,
my hero, my mentor, without hearing him call me
his little girl, without my Daddy, I am alone.

God, I blame you for the desolation I see
inside me, the unimpeded lashing out of arrows
without care where they land, who they pierce
because I am bereft, my soul is alone.

God, forgive me for forgetting that, though sorrow
fills me to bursting with hurt, I repent that I've fallen
victim to blaming, remind me that with you in my heart
I am never alone.

Along the Way to Christmas Dinner

a squirrel skitters
halfway across the street
his companion continues
he stops, hesitates
in front of our SUV
we both brake
he turns, we stop
we're both saved
        Merry Christmas

* * * * *

Alphabetapillar

a bear cub
doesn't eat
fat grizzly hogs
instead just kids,
little morsels
not overly porcine,
quite readily seized
tasty unseasoned vittles
without xtraneous yeasty zones

Alteration

it began as a whimsical whisper
an insistent susurrus mantra *now*
now now time for action, time for change

time to admit you're aching to shed your shell
your armor, your reticence and reveal to the world
your need to birth a revolution
no more self-doubt, no more distractions

with a soldier's abandon, you attack the closet
rid yourself of all disguises
all false innuendo, all too-small ideas

ready for boldness and bravado,
for wearing yellow to compete with the sun
you pack up the too-tight, too-trendy, too-
something that makes you look fat
cart the bags to the local donation bin
and applaud yourself inside a closet
that echoes with emptiness
        you celebrate with a glass of Merlot

and it begins again as a whisper
now now now
time to clean out your shoe collection
including the stash under the bed
the ones you're hiding from your husband
but can't hide from your conscience

but you're strong, smart, resourceful
you can tackle any job, large or small
and you stifle that whimpy whispering voice
        with dark decadent chocolate

leave my shoes alone, bitch

Alternative Cycle

his moods threaded to the new moon, he marks
his calendar with a red X, locks himself in
for a straightjacket night; he's a landslide of changeability
at just the wrong right time, a single moonray sprouts
tufts of invincibility on lined face, on forearms bulging
with a lifetime of crops harvested for pennies
on the dollar, but that's not the problem

his eyes shade to evergreen envy
when he thinks of the silver spooners
who'll be two-stepping with his Lucy
the sweetest thing in all of Carver County
who'd never two-time him, never give up
on him even if he couldn't spend Saturday night
with her, pretending he was sick again

he blames the calendar, tide changing time for him
to stay in, stay home, stay away from Lucy –
a quick check on the horses in the barn
ah, a luminous ray bullets his hand
he's cliffside with wanting to go
tilt a few back before he sees her pickup
turn the corner towards his driveway

he remembers last May and shutters himself
inside his house, clicks the locks, the dead bolt,
transforming hands to his face, he crumbles
weeping on the floor, sobs through the door
for Lucy to go away and instead of her
takes a bottle of bourbon
to bed till morning

Alternatives

                I can't decide
should I move the red nine to the black ten
or the black five to the red six
the order of moves could make all the difference.

                I can't decide
should I have salmon crusted with honey dijon
or the prime rib au jus
my heartburn after could make all the difference.

                I can't decide
should I wear the amethyst wedge boots
or the purple pencil-heel pumps
my soles sore tonight could make all the difference.

                I can't decide
should I get him a new cell phone
or the dress shirts he needs
my birthday gift choice could make all the difference.

                I can't decide
should I stay on the highway
or turn off for a scenic ride
my diverging could make all the difference.

Always Blowing

In a house of wind, blinds billow
in a house of wind, drapes dance
in a house of wind, doors and windows
tapdance open, calypso closed
tango a bass beat for attics to mimic,
for basements to secret. In a house of wind,
decibels drown out the Zeppelin cd,
fly up the table skirt, down the staircase,
gust dust from the bedroom bureau,
zephyr stacks of unfinished poems
to hover on fan blades.
In a house of wind, bank statements stewardess
from sofa to love seat, land on a runway
of tornado soil, the dog digging up houseplants.
In a house of wind, books preen feathers,
arch bindings to soar over the piano,
play polkas on chandelier crystals,
peck words like worms from the dictionary,
definitions too fat to fly. In our house of wind,
promises catch in cobweb corners,
lies hide under carpets, questions propose
a tempest; conversations lost in the din,
we huddle together under a blanket of silence.

Amandacized

Amanda will not leave my head
thirteen, blazing hair, wire-rimmed grey eyes
a rail of a spitfire; a prodigy
not ashamed, adamant even that it's okay
that she can't write.

I don't mean purple prose
or prolific paragraphs of potential Pulitzers.
I mean script; round curly, loopy lines that spell out
Education.

"It is, after all" her lip curls, cheeks flame
"*Now.* I haven't scripted anything since the third grade
and why should I anyhow. I have a laptop and a text-
messaging phone to keep me in touch, up-to-date with
Now."

Useless I see to explain that SATs require script
not just kinder-print, but I'm just the proctor
reading directions, overseeing no cheating zones –
her spittle stings my faith in learning.

I mind-travel ahead five years. How will she sign
a college app, a credit card receipt, endorse a check?
Is she unique
or have our future chemists and doctors and lawyers
and say-it-ain't-so *teachers* become Amandacized?

"Get with the program,"
she spits.
Get out of my head, Amanda.
Now.

AMEN

       Amen, amen I say to you...
       Men of good will...
       Everything in its time...
       No prayer goes unheard...
Always trust in the Lord, that His plan is greater than you,
greater than your wants by length and breadth a thousand fold...
but as a galaxy of stars is brightest with all shining together,
know that God needs you to polish up your flaws, repent your greed
and self-need, step onto the stage with all your neighbors and trust
that you will be redeemed for blessed are the clean of heart
for they shall see God.

Make amends as you will have others make amends to you
without waiting for someone else to make the effort, start the cycle
of friendship turning, let the truth ring out, your voice sing out
the praises of the Lord, repent and pray for mercy for your remorse
and your sins be forgiven, your mistrust to die crushed beneath
the weight of your penance, heartfelt, pious, and trusting that God
trusts you to do right. Don't let Him down.

Every man is your brother, every stranger a friend waiting
to be accepted. Be kind and giving, yet wary as the devil decks himself
in vainglory, beckons the weak of faith to join him. Be cautious
as the devil steals souls never forgives or relents. In God's hands,
if you stumble, He catches you, rights you, holds you, wipes your tears
of confession with redemption. He sends you friends who help guide
you with angel wings. Trust in Him.

Never wish for another's life or possessions,
for you cannot know what lies hidden beneath the outward veneer,
what secrets are camouflaged under the mask of daily life. Learn
from challenges, reflect on your actions, and practice knee-mail
not just on Sunday but every day. Live within God's arms
and you will always rest gentle against his chest, nearest
to his Sacred Heart.

       Amen, amen I say to you...
       Men of good will...
       Everything in its time...
       No prayer goes unheard...

America On Wheels
    Levittown Arena

Take a ride down Hempstead Turnpike, really East Meadow
and not Levittown, though I only know that now –
there's a trendy Mexican restaurant I've never had a yen to visit,
beside it a sleek glass-and-brick faced bank with a massive green TD
like a beacon calling for savings. Tucked into a corner, a designer
warehouse for shoes I'm going to frequent often someday.

But I don't see these modernistic marvels of architecture. Rippling,
like heat from blacktop streets, a concrete building, soaring curved roof
and no windows specters before Mex, the shoe store, the levitating TD
fading beside the rise of Jahn's Ice Cream Parlor, behind the
mausoleum of oval rink, ringed by a short wall, then circled with bench
chairs lined with sneakers, penny-loafers, mary-janes and saddle-shoes.

I rise above this crypt, hover at the cathedral-scaled ceiling where
speakers blare organ music orchestrating hundreds of two-by-two
wheels on a wood floor, witness to the cyclical partings of girls and
guys, a dazzling disco-ball dropping with the lights for "couples only,"
for hand-in-hand, arm-in-arm turns around the rink, chaperoned by
maroon suit-and-hat "Clippers" guarding safe skating. The rink opened
in 1955, closed in 1986, but this memory reel is from 1977.

Surreptitious smiles, giggles, circling, spinning, skate-dancing swagger,
you race to slow beside me, turn to face me, pace me, entice me to
follow, to leave the safe cocoon of my girlfriends, to unlace the white
pom-pom skates on loan from my mother, and go with you. So
pompous, so confident, so sure I would take your hand and skate past
my innocence – good-Catholic girl upbringing, coy love of flirtations,
the purgatory of sending my heart one message, my mind another.

Today, I saw you in Walmart – summer-streaked chestnut hair gone,
frown creases replaced your easy smile, the blaze in your slate eyes
doused to dull grey. If you saw me, and I'll never know, no flicker of
recognition, no threshold of expression birthed from you as you
shuffleboarded by me.

You, a specter of our past, a specter kept alive in me until now,
when I let you go, let the vision on Hempstead Turnpike
ripple to a long dead tomb.

American Tapestry
after Collage (of the same name) by Hedi Flickstein
in tribute to Walt Whitman

Stars and bars, white lines of freedom,
crimson stripes of bloodshed,
blue field of *orbs of night dappled,* rippling waves
over oceans of peace and war and peace again
> *flag of teeming life!*

babes and toddlers, children, teens
mothers fathers, brothers sisters
aunts uncles and grandparents
friends, strangers, and neighbors
> sing America!

salesmen and janitors in uniform voices
bricklayers in mortar choral, clerks
and cashiers in bells ringing, sanitation crews
clanging melodious cans in early morn –
> sing America!

tailors hum to threaded needle hymns
cell phone tunes embracing friendship
radios play for comrades arm-in-arm
to sway in peaceful circles
> sing America!

truck haulers and taxi drivers in red rays
of dawn/dusk light obeying white lines
of roadway laws beneath a ceiling
of everlasting blue
> *flag cerulean!*

thick-sprinkled bunting! field of heavenly stars,
a new constellation
"The New Colossus" crowning our Lady Liberty,
torch held high, head held high,
your Lady, Walt,
> *my matron mighty!*

erected in stony battle roars for freedom
in drum-taps, soldier taps and they tramp through
Manhattan *(my own, my peerless!)* down to the river
guns on shoulders, marching with pride for peace
    my sacred one, my mother
eyes watching over our beloved Paumanok,
"Liberty Enlightening the World" arm stretched
to draw back the darkness, the curtain of enslavement
to welcome the tired, the poor, the "huddled masses..."
    my matron mighty!
yearning to breathe free..."
flag, our flag, we salute you
you salute us by waving back
    Flag of death!
draped over eternal rest, folded 13 times
each fold symbolic: 1st for life; 2nd for belief in eternal life;
3rd to honor and remember veterans; 4th for our weaker nature,
turning to His Divine nature in times of peace and times of war;
5th in tribute to our country;
6th where our hearts lie, with our hearts we Pledge Allegiance
to the Flag of the United States of America, and to the Republic
for which it stands, one Nation under God, indivisible, with
Liberty and Justice for All –
(for you, Walt – our Pledge published
    less than six months after your death) –
7th fold a tribute to our Armed Forces to protect us and our Flag;
8th in tribute to the one who entered into the valley of the shadow
of death, that we might see the light of day; 9th a tribute to
womanhood; 10th a tribute to fatherhood;
    ah my wooly white and crimson!
11th in tribute to Hebrew God of Abraham, Isaac, and Jacob;
12th in tribute to Christian God the Father, Son, and Holy Ghost;
13th final fold reminds us "In God We Trust" –
flag of life, flag of liberty, *flap and rustle, cloth defiant!*
    flag of America!

Amish Carpenter
      Farmer's Market, Pennsylvania

If it's not being nosey
what happened to your mailbox?

      Nothing.

Really? No kids roughousin' with it?

      No.

A snowplow knock it down? We had
an almanac bad blizzard this past winter...

      No.

Hmmm, the wife miscalculate the driveway
maybe need a new pair 'a glasses?

      Uhh, no.

Not that I don't make a fine mailbox.
Looky here, tight seams, quality hinge,
solid post. Actual barn red paint, too.
Are ya moving?

      Nope. Just getting a new one.

Well pickle me in pigs feet. And there's nothing
wrong with the old one?

      Nothing.

You're from New Yalk, right?
Are you one of them Rockefellers?

An American Czech

"Chcete pivo?" The second thing she taught me
to say in Czech. "You need to be able to ask him
if he wants a beer. It's a wife's duty."

He's an American and speaks English and besides,
he can get his own beer
but I don't tell her this.

She's an American, but she mixes her heritage
like she mixes her slovakian stew
a little of this, a little of that.

"Dobre." The third thing she taught me to say
because everything will be *good*
when I know how to ask him if he wants a beer.

"Yak se mas?" she asks me
her tan, freckled face tilted
her bohemian eyes glinting like rain-washed slate.

"Dobre." I'm *good*. I'm an American
learning to marry the son of an American Czech.
Everything *is dobre*.

The first thing she taught me
"Miluji te."
I love her, too.

An Apple A Day

A fellow writer, this fellow who writes
told me that his mother has had an apple a day
for the past thirty years

Such an inspiration   "Write it!" I tell him

Imagine the devotion, the loyalty, the love of apples
to have one every single day
every single year for thirty years

I wonder
does she
slice it, quarter it, dice it
or eat it whole, one big delicious bite at a time
pick out the seeds, plant them to have a home-grown supply

is she devoted to one variety
MacIntosh, Granny Smith, Empire, Fuji
Ginger Gold, Honeycrisp, Jonagold
or Newtown Pippin, our Long Island own, circa 1759

does she alternate
depending on what her son
brings her every two weeks

has she ever missed a day
did she feel unwell
waiting for the doctor to visit

Such an inspiration   "Write it!" I tell myself

But perhaps when I do
I'll substitute a pear for an apple
Bartlett, Seckel, Bosc, Anjou ...

An Integral Difference

a cat curls into a corner,
into a bed, into the cleft of your heart

a comma curls around items in a listing,
sets off quoted elements, avoids confusion

a cat curls on a curtain rod, on the dog,
on your head when you are at rest

a comma curls with a conjunction
to connect independent clauses, pauses
          after an interjection – oh,

a cat uses whiskers to navigate and to measure
distance; they are as long as the cat is wide
          never cut a cat's receptors

an address uses a comma to divide city,
and state; month, date, and year

an integral difference –
a cat and a comma

one has claws
at the ends of its paws

the other is a pause
at the end of a clause

An Untold Tale

After seven years and a bottle of wine,
Snow White finished her memoirs.
Seventy chapters strewn with chores,
picking up after seven little men of simple songs;
after long days of solitude that ended when
the elfin pack returned for supper,
seven tinny voices vying for her attention,
for her *ooohs* and *ahhhs,* for her acceptance
of a male-dominant household,
she read them her manuscript.
They *hmphed* and huffed
and locked her in the pantry;
she needed to get free, to get out,
to get a publisher. She finally slipped away,
slipped through the seven four-poster beds
tip-toed through bulbous nose snores,
out the door to a pathway through the forest
to a sturdy brick house with double-pane windows;
she peeked in to see three whiny little pigs
on wing-back chairs, cloven hooves resting
on ottomans, cigars sprouting
from their snouted mouths.
She knocked and knocked;
they didn't answer.
Somewhere she'd find a publisher,
perhaps down the mountain to a tidy house
smoke billowing through a chimney,
gardens greeting her with warmth,
the door open, a cauldron boiling
on the fireplace, a young girl screaming
down the hall, the gnashing of razor teeth
in a wolf face below a floral night cap;
she ran and ran, right into three billy goats,
who *naaaahed* her to cross a bridge,
where a swampy-skinned troll danced,

delighting in her fright; she turned around,
pushed the goats to the ground
and ran into the night.
Morning light woke her on the steps of a castle,
where she found a glass slipper
she slipped on her foot. Royal trumpets summoned
the prince who whisked her up the stone steps,
pledging marriage and everlasting happiness,
but no publisher for her book.
After seven years of nagging,
he locked her in a tower, let her hair grow
as long as eternity. She tied her book pages
to the ends of her tresses, tossed it out of the tower
to land at the base of the castle.
A long wooden nose appeared, eventually
a wooden boy attached to it; she begged him
to take her book to the nearest Doubleday office
but Pinocchio took it home to read, his nose
growing longer each time he said
he'd written it himself,
until it was stolen by a pair of grim-faced brothers.
They got an agent, a movie deal, and are living
on an island off the Caribbean,
researching pirate legends.
Snow White is working on her second novel
about two evil stepsisters
and a princess in disguise.
She is searching for a publisher
with a very long ladder.

Anatomy of a Nightmare

spine of slivered shards
arms of ephemeral mist
that cloy and cling to elusive dust

legs that sink in cemetery soil
to knees that refuse to bend

torso twists in gnarled effigies
of evil flames of intent

rope-burned hands grasp at shadows
silent scream scars the throat

eyes coffined against tunnel light
endless chase of dreamscape

ears blasted by moaning,
wailing, shrieking siren
divine alarm that calls me back

                     from the cadaver of sleep

And She's Not Blonde

she's sharp as a bowling ball
bright as a starless night
she's quick as honey, clever as a cell phone that's off
alert as a bat in sunlight

she's a wickless lump of wax
she's an everyday waste of makeup
she's got that deer-in-the-headlight look   all the time
when her computer says she has mail,
        she stands by her mailbox
she thinks Cheerios are donut seeds
when the phone rings, she answers the door
when a tire goes flat, she keeps driving
        because she has three more

when her computer goes to sleep,
        she covers it with a blanket
when she gets her doctor's bill, she mails him an apple
when her mechanic billed her for signal fluid,
        she thanked him and paid it

she believes pushing the button
        will actually change traffic lights
she went to the forest to find her family tree
she sued the candy company
        for putting W's in the M&M's bag
she has more fun but doesn't remember
she hangs out with brunettes hoping ...
she thinks the capital of Nevada is 'N'
she smiles at lightning, thinks someone is taking her picture

to change her mind, blow in her ear
to keep her busy all day, on both sides of a paper
        write "Please turn over"
to keep her in suspense,
        well, I'll tell you tomorrow ...

And Suddenly...

but there is no such thing as suddenly
nothing happens in a flash
flood of stopped time, lightning storm
harbingered by meteorologists, by thunder
brings an arm-hair senses-alert warning
to prepare.

You need to prepare
to understand there is no suddenly
no ah-ha of insight without a warning
no poetic inspirations in a photoflash
no curtain falling final act without thunder
-ous applause before house lights storm

on, hammer and nail crew storm
the stage; unprop, undress, unprepare
for the next show, next drove to thunder
in for the matinee, tickets paid, no suddenly
to see a movie/show in a driving flash
thinking, planning, everything a warning.

Tendrils of curling smoke before bonfire warning
for gas can holders to step away from roaring storm
flames that creep and grow, send a tangerine flash
to shadow pyros to change their ways, prepare
to not play with matches, though nothing suddenly
will change them, even the bruised sound of thunder.

No suddenly as a stampede of elephants thunder
to the Big Top, always a carload of clowns warning
the Big Show is about to start, big days unsuddenly
rolling out before you in a carnival calendar storm
of possibilities, opportunities for you to prepare
before the end of the line, end of days ends in a flash

and you're sobbing in darkness without a flash
-light of insight as the pearly stockades thunder

open, your mentors, your guides there to prepare
you – there's no need for fear, no need for warning
no descent downstairs to a brimstone storm
because your arrival happened unsuddenly.

I give you this, a pseudo-flashcard warning:
Thunder through life, blaze your own storm
revel, laugh, live; prepare for nothing suddenly.

    (Sestina)

* * * * *

And Yet Without It

Poetry is the salt in the sea
        an empty seat on a train, two ladybugs on a leaf
Poetry is the hole of a donut
        the pitch of a piano, sand at the beach
Poetry is the sound of patience
        the wick of a candle, feathers falling from a nest
Poetry is the moment inside a minute
        the phasing of phrases, fragments of a fraction
the molecular structure of DNA without the N
        a slivered glance, an unfinished sonata
a speck   a shard   the trace of an iota
        a hole in my heart that leaks through my pen
Poetry is but a part
        and yet without it ...

Angels of War

battle weary, slumped with discouragement
they rest in roadbeds beside streets scarlet slick with greed

they wait in basements crowded with innocence
consoling crestfallen grief for souls lost to bomb blasts of hatred

they huddle on closet floors, comforting women
hiding to survive sacrificial maiming, torture, mutilation, rape

they question why a thousand times a moment

they no longer fly, wings overwrought with sorrow
feathers fatigue grey, limp, dispirited, shedding rubble rife with rancor

they cannot cry, anguished tears long dried on cheeks
overlaid with grit, they pray for understanding, resolution, redemption

they cannot leave until carnivores of war are destroyed
minions of murderers captured, sentenced to rot in cells of hell

their duty, though they wish the word war was never born

they've been here before, different country, different weapons,
different excuse for conflict, the same slaying, carnage, killing, death

when peace reigns, these angels will rise, pristine feathers preened
guarding our world until the next call to arms, soldiers, angels of war

Angry Poem

what else to call it
when words come in blood welts, raw and open
to infectious fury, every smile a criticize, every wink
disguised to hide malice, silence a raging storm
a boiling tempest building hostile irritation
into a steaming vortex

what else is there
when words come spitting bitter vile
spiteful biting rabid words aimed to maim, bred to cripple
you disappear in an enraged red cloud of resentment
wrathful retorts spewed fuming, blazing with contempt
leave me feeling pointless, hopeless, no damn good

frontier of apologies cuffed behind steel doors
cowering in dark corners of remorse
callous, we feed them disdain
they remain impassive
too powerless to resist complacent
too arrogant to move to the light

what else to do
when pleasant words won't come
but purge them on paper, porous to absorb
granules of hate, freeing us to cross thresholds
of contrition, linen or parchment
reconciliation on wrinkled sheets

Anniversary
for Ron

Drifting from the dining room
traversing staircases, hallways
fragrance greets me
making the bed
doing dishes, laundry
vacuuming, writing
taps me on the shoulder
lures me to stand at the table

stargazers large as dinner plates
surround white, peach
yellow, lavender lilies
a mint-green glazed vase
delivered with a box of chocolates
cellophane sealed
waiting to be savored

inhale intensity
eyes closed
thinking of you
our 9th anniversary
not nuptials
yet a shared love

a date written in friendship
perfume sweet as memories
this beckoning scent
will forever
remind me
of you

Anniversary Shopping

After twenty-nine years of bliss
a place they can go together
parting ways inside the orange doors.

Like a starving man, he follows the scent
of sawdust, pliant as putty, flexible as luan,
he molds himself into dreams

of pressure-treated decking, a double-doored
storage shed with a bay window, a ten-horse
lawn tractor with pivoting headlights and nubuck leather seat

but first he needs to clear the trees in the backyard forest,
to weed and seed the lawn, maybe even put in a hot tub
for their thirtieth anniversary.

Yes, the best place for him –
a do-it-yourself warehouse
for the handy, whole-hearted dreamer.

They arrange to be home tomorrow
to take delivery of the new washer, dryer and microwave
and the spring clean-up special chainsaw/chipper shredder.

For her, the hot tub will be a surprise next week;
for him, the side-by-side split freezer-door fridge
with automatic ice and water.

Yes, a shared joy
shopping together
in Home Depot.

Annual Maelstrom

Twas the day of first warming
and all through our home
termites were swarming
we weren't alone!

We opened the windows
threw up each sash
hoping the wind blow
would blow out this trash.

They swarmed in the living room
through the kitchen and then
flew into the dining room
and on to our den.

My sister, how she cried
my brother how he giggled
as we stood to the side
watching a cloud that wriggled.

They'll spelled out "hello"
as they droned in our ear
then they flew out the window
waving "See you next year!"

another lost earring

   ... ahh

  a new pendant

      (Senryu)

* * * *

      another pen
      out of ink
      too much writing –
      ha! like that's possible...

    (Senryu)

* * * *

another summer
   c a r r i e d o f f
with autumn leaves

    (Haiku)

anything is possible
if you bury the word
impossible

(Senryu)

* * * * *

aphids invade buds
ladybugs to the rescue:
the pure white rose tips

(Haiku)

* * * * *

apocolipstick
dynamite red lips
too dangerous to kiss

(Senryu)

* * * * *

apples
60 varieties in produce section
which one to pick…

(Senryu)

April

Our front yard Frosty disappeared months ago;
where he stood sentinel over frigid mounds
now there are daffodils and hyacinths
quenched by his melting.

His accouterments disappeared as well;
his carrot nose carted off by a squirrel,
his twig arms flighted by birds,
but I wondered where
his cardinal hat and scarf had gone

until today, the first warm winds
summoning me to inspect the gardens,
assess ravages of winter's cruelty
and I see a crimson-something
in the crook of the dogwood.

Pom-pom side down, the hat sat
wreathed by twigs and leaves, the scarf
wrapped like a bungee around limbs
for stability, tassels waving me closer.

Parents-to-be hovered on overhead wires
while I crept closer, documenting the image
to build a poem around –
I think of Frosty and how his memory lives
in a nest of flame red yarn
reborn to warm baby birds in spring.

Architect

My desk – swimming in a sea of sun-soaked poems
tanned, half-tanned, and scorched
to angry red, I push them together
into a neat pile of white pages –
I fashion an island out of paper.

The fanned border is fragrant with sunburst petals
peeking through palm fronds alive with bird calls,
soft warm wind whispers my name,
alabaster sand flecked with purple shells
surround a turquoise cove of tranquil water.

In the center, a volcano of mismatched, balled-up
tossed-off insipid poems that grumble
their discontent, roil with contemptuous envy
at hibiscus and fern, crops of coconuts
and voluptuous mangoes intimating plush pulp.

These outcasts threaten to rumble together,
spew their disjointed views into a thunderclap
of images raining down, crushing tender buds,
cleaving tropical vines, pouring a lava of demonic
lines to ashen all in charcoal death throes.

Quickly, I level the island, divide the pile –
formed - unformed, finished - unfinished,
liquid silver platinum from blemished lead
treasure from trash, stacking to separate them
with a wall I build of books.

Subdivide - organize, careful not to cause a war of words
in mixed metaphor; aligning corners, I pour a foundation
of robust images, frame a structure of stable rafters, roof
each pile with a punctuated promise to love them all.
Fabrications complete, peace reigns on my desk once more.

Argument

They sit mannequin still
at a side table
in the Wyld Chyld Café.

He slouches in slashed-knee jeans
black button-down over silk-screened tee
printed with something I can't see.

It may be his rakish black hat
shadowing his face, but he seems aloof
disinterested by anything she may have to say.

Chiseled features serene, she's poised
shoulders back, knees together,
feet Ms Manners flat on the floor.

Her spaghetti-straight raven hair
spills from her avant-garde hat, not a strand
strays from her vampire pale face as we crowd in

for a poetry reading. Actually, neither one blinks
as we fill tables and chairs with journals, pages
of printed verse we're anxious to share

with our new audience, but we go unnoticed.
No tea or coffee, no cookie, cake, ice cream
on their table, and I wonder why they're here,

wonder why her left hand levitates
as though waiting for him to hold it, squeeze it
promise to fill the void on her ring finger

or maybe she's readying to cock her palm
elegant wind-up to smack his smug face
and put an end to their silent argument.

Argument Viewed at the Photo Booth

Your fingers are not my photo album
swirled prints mar the corners of features
smudge colors to whirl in distant dimension,
dropping images at the finish.

My past is not yours to store
on a living room coffee table
to push before guests, before drinks,
before dinner of take-out Italian,
before they realize
your journeys have been glossed over,
reprinted in five by seven lies,
varnished on pages pulping fiction.

Let me be candid; get yourself a life;
my life, my prints, my memories
are not for the taking;
                         they're mine alone to process.

Arlington National Cemetery

Tomb of the Unknowns
      white Yule Marble engraved
            with wreaths and Peace, Victory, and Valor
Tomb Guards, The Old Guard
      US Army's 3rd Infantry Regiment
            80% of soldiers who try out are not chosen

elite standards required
      for duty of eternal vigilance
            secured 24/7 since 1937
walking the mat, a 63 foot rubber walkway
      patrol is 21 steps, with a 21 second pause
            to face the Tomb, a turn, a 21 second pause

before resuming a 21 step return
      perfect repetition, the highest salute
            for these fallen heroes Unknown but not forgotten.
"Here Rests In Honored Glory
      An American Soldier Known But To God."
            loaded M14 rifle points away from the Tomb

silent sentry prevents invasion
      of four graves – WWI, WWII, Korea, Vietnam –
            crypts to hold Unknown remains

            one grave is vacant

Vietnam Unknown identified
      Air Force 1st Lt Michael Joseph Blassie
            shot down near An Loc, Vietnam in 1972

DNA analysis confirmed
      remains disinterred in 1998
            crypt remains empty, Army Blue remains
in humble reverence
      may there never be another Unknown
            may the memorial remain a reminder of our past

    through all seasons, patrols
        render honors before The Tomb:
            11 foot high, 8 foot wide marble monument
    guarding against intrusion
        to three esteemed Unknowns
            Rest in Peace, rest assured

    the vigil will continue
        unhindered, unaltered, undefeated
            led by The Tomb Guards, versed
    by the 99 words of The Sentinel's Creed
        saluting superiors, saying, "Line six, Sir!"

            My standard will remain perfection.

Art of the Bargain

George lives directly across the street
keeps a constant eye on our home
monitors our comings/goings with concern
for early morning/late hours out
are we getting enough sleep
how are the dogs, is there anything we need.

He lost his wife a number of years ago
a collector of all things eclectic/eccentric
exotic, Helen never wanted for a thing
George couldn't find a way to get her;
he still mourns her, strives to fill his days   without her.

He's our favorite neighbor, considerate
beyond words, generous beyond measure
and the grand master of a bargain.
Spring through autumn, he's up and out
early Saturday mornings, cruising
the yard/garage/estate sales to rummage up
the best deals on nicknacks/paddywacks
foundlings in need of a good home.

He's an amazing negotiator to seal the deal
with seller/buyer smiles, but that's the take
for George; he doesn't want stuff –
he wants to buy stuff too good to pass up.
SUV hatch and backseat jingling with transient
treasures, he takes the long way home, stopping
here/there/where he knows a heart's desire
to deliver unwrapped Santa gifts in offseason splendor.

Though I'm the last stop on his journey home
he often pops the back and saunters across
to my front porch, leaving glittery trinkets
to make my heart glow, make his eyes dance
make me love my bargain hunting neighbor   even more.

Artistry

gold
old gold
intricate carvings
like facets
catch light
that burst from it

one of a pair
once worn by royalty
saved from scavengers
hidden from warmongers

lost for generations
found in a thrift store
their legacy unknown
their heritage masked
their worth disguised
beneath a patina of neglect

I found it hanging
on a cheap velvet stand
its twin fallen to the floor
it mocked the costumed price tag

felt regal holding it
felt like a queen trying them on
felt like a thief buying them

they dangle from my earlobes
whisper crowned secrets to me
their legacy treasured

(Drabble)

As Poets

As poets, we are like farmers
planting seeds to root in rich loam
amending to create nutrients
      to nourish hungry souls
cultivating words, coaching blossoms
      beyond gardens of our lives.

As poets, we are like contractors
building metaphor as a sound foundation
firm walls to hang similes from brass hooks
      landscapes framed in oiled oak
thresholds to welcome weary travelers
      to unburden from daily baggage.

As poets, we are like cobblers
stitching crafted seams in fine lines
heeling at mundane, solid soles to step
      lightly over emotion
lacing tangents in silvered streams of memory
      to comfort those in need.

As poets, we are like musicians
strumming chords into contentment
like pharmacists filling scripts
      to heal hurts, cure aches
basket makers weaving willow thin strands
      to carry us into tomorrow.

As people, we are like poets
travel agents giving guided tours
map makers, fulfilling our destinies
      to touch the world
with words
      our work never done.

Ashes to Ashes

I am dust, carry dust of Irish immigrants
wear dust of toil-back labor, I eat dust
for breakfast, ash sprinkled on oatmeal
soot on white with mayo, a bowl of embers
with oyster crackers dusting the surface,
dust of dead flesh marbleized with dust fat
and marinated in a vinaigrette of cinders.

I am dust of lazy, dust of maple dining table
dust of murky mirrors, of grungy windows
dust of parched plants, of attic lost yearnings
dust of basement buried hopes, dust of tears
dust of strangers I know who clutched
at crumbling towers to smack me
into remembering my American pride.

I am dust, choke on dust, smoke dust
famished by dust, dream dust, rooftop dust
boiled desert dust, seed dust sprouting
from moth wing dust carried on a north
by northeasterly dust breeze to alight
on dust, spark flame dust, settle in
for the dusty long haul, fall down
to grave dust.

At Her Reading

a poet stands with books stacked
like an altar behind her
inspirations before her
laid out on a garden path
that wends around white birch
bark, a trail of pebbled soil strewn
with fallen acorns, wild violets
and frothy ferns
oak limbs canopy above
as she guides us through thickets
of briars and brambles
past columns of tulip trees
and clumps of vibrant moss
that flank the banks of a pond

no boards below us, no oars to steer us
we plunge forward into creative waters
emerge cleansed of our judgments
shaking off droplets
we yearn for another submerging
at the baptism
of her next poem

At My Demise

When I get to the Pearly Gates
St. Peter will have a clipboard list
of every murder I've ever committed

and I'll have to answer for them all
beginning with the big black ant
that roamed the hills of my comforter

in search of Sammy the Bear perched
on my pillow, smashing the intruder
with my bare hand back when I was five

and countless wasps, worms, mosquitos
that have hounded me since, crickets
in our basement, yellow-jackets in the walls

but never spiders as my grandmother swore
if you killed a spider in your home
you'd lose money, so spiders were spared.

Now carpenter bees bore through our awning
our deck, nesting in dozens of hidden havens
droning, hovering, antagonizing our dogs.

Four empty cans of insecticide and a swarm
of inert belly-up bodies litter our deck and still
droves far-from-extinct buzz in my face
	...and I wonder if I'll ever even *meet* St. Peter.

At the Academy Awards

Fading starlet dreams
of plump lips
perky breasts
greater-than-Gable legs.

Competition is fierce
with 20-something trim figures
slender sequined waists
décolletage dresses
no need for imaginings
sleek slinky fabrics
with no bulges to disguise
and tower tall heels
without a wobble.

Botox creates Houdini illusions
that fade in bright sunlight
but under the paparazzi spotlights
suggestive shadows hollow cheekbones
carrion-red lips distract
just enough for a flash
as she sashays in the red-carpet parade.

Too many tucks nipped
and snipped again
until nerve endings
wave a surgical white flag
stubborn not to stretch
not to move a facial muscle –
that's when the fading starlet's dream
morphs to be a busty Charlie McCarthy
on Edgar Bergen's lap.

At the Death of Winter

We watch from windows
wet with warming tears
see the cease of gales
scourged on bitter land
witness bare limbs hang
with humility, have faith
savior rains will fall, carry away
agony of frozen gardens
quench roots of bone-dry beds
birth worms and bees to duty
heal hands of scarred stems
hold hope in a passionate embrace
encourage bulbs, bushes, trees
to burst forth in choruses of
Alleluia
rejoice, arise in resurrection
behold a miracle
five pink blossoms
on an azalea branch
at the birth of spring.

At the stroke of midnight

kidnapped by an ogre in chartreuse skin
breath sewer rat rancid
huge as a mountain, tucked to his chest
we leapt into the night, flew to his lair

cold, damp cave walls slime slick
I'm dropped to a bone-littered floor –
he leans in, spittle flies
"I love to murder, need to murder
gonna murder you"

retching from his stench
face milliseconds from mine
I gag, ask his preferred method of murder
hope to stall death, hold out for a miracle

he sneers
"roasting is most tasty"

my laugh is maniacal
I flick my bic and he's aflame
"my preference, too"

(Drabble)

At-Home Stress Relief

I was feeling a bit stressed
and called Tech Support
told the geek who muttered *yeah?*
that the crankshaft in my printer
threw a rod, was leaking oil
and I needed a repairman to fix it.
He asked me if I had any software spots
on top of my head because I needed to call
a mechanic,
and so I asked him if he repaired
mechanical things, like computers,
and when he mumbled *yeah*,
I informed him that he was a mechanic
and that's why the heck I was calling.

After an exasperated sigh
that lasted a full minute,
he told me to open the printer
and push the silver thingamajig
to the right and I did,
and that's when he told me put
my finger under the doohickey
that looks like a whatchamacallit,
only sideways, and pull,
and in his evil-robot voice,
chuckled repair was complete,
not covered under my warranty,
and the $135 charge would be billed
to my credit card.

I asked if he had any loose screws
rattling around in the space his brain
should occupy because if he did,
he needed to call a handyman,

and that's when I informed him
that I just broke a nail
because my finger was caught
in the hoosiewhatsit
and here's where I really let lose,
man, the sawdust was flying
like my brain was a lathe
and this geek-hole
was a scrap of termite-infested lumber.

So, do you have a PhD
in computer repair
or are you a blob of fat and plasma
hoarding skin that could be used as grafts,
or a brainless, worthless waste
sucking up our precious air?
He called me a bad name
that ended in blonde and hung up.
My stress meter went down,
I felt better. Now,
who to call next?

Augmentation

She's a comma
waiting to grow into something
more than a pause, more than a connector
between clauses, more than a separation
between sentence elements.

She's got a good head on her shoulders;
round, firmly packed with knowledge
of grammatic structure and deconstruction
of syntactic patterns; her timing is a half-
second sooner than her half-cousin, the period.

From below her head, the curve of her neck
to her toes shows she is not adverse to inflections,
flexible to modifications in phonemics,
phraseologies, and versed in the key roles of
coordinate and subordinate clauses.

She's a comma, the analytical type
with a BA in serial placement, and a PhD
in linguistic science, trained in stratificational
grammar, transformational grammar,
and universal tagmemics.

At times, she finds herself underrated,
the apostrophe doppelganger hovering
over her shoulder in mock dominance,
mostly misused, misplaced, mistaken;
she's gratified her usage is generally correct.

She hates to be replaced by a colon,
that double-dotted prequel preceding a listing,
or the repeated hyphen, that blankety-blank dash
of insolence she so despises;
she's qualified to replace them both.

She's a comma
with ambitious dreams, buoyant aspirations,
growing to her goal to rise above her steady line;
she's waiting, she's hoping, she's a semicolon
in the making.

August 31, 2008

Sunday, we get up, shower, dress
get to church on time, we pray
and sometime after church
the aliens came in an invisible ship
carted us off to brainwash us

make us forget negative things
like waking every hour to howls
and whimpers, letting them out
and coaxing them back to sleep
and of course, forget the messes
only to remember the good things
like tail-wagging, sloppy wet kisses
being met at the door with enthusiasm
at our return, even if after a trip
to the mailbox, warm bodies in a cold bed

we must have hovered overhead
before they put us in my truck
and directed us to North Shore Animal League
where they locked the door behind us
said we couldn't leave
until we adopted another puppy,
rescued another homeless orphan,
until we saved another life

that's the story of how it happened
and we're sticking to it.

August Days

August is a hot glass of winter ice
streets are crossed streams of steaming tar
that seize soles of sneakers; I duck into the cool shadows

of the hardware store. From behind the counter,
my father smiles, counting out change to ancient Mrs Gray;
mothballs in hand, she passes; I giggle and say "Good day,"

approach the tall, burly man I call Daddy.
We chat, swiping sweat from our brows;
smiles and a can of soda pass between us.

He inspects his hands before looking at me.
My father wants to know what secrets I hide inside,
what lurks behind the whispered words of mother and daughter,

sequestered chats swallowed in silence at his arrival;
what keeps her away all day, until dinner serves us
warm egg salad and weak lemonade.

In another town, a man I wish I didn't know
runs smooth young fingers down her breast,
caresses her sweat-stained cheeks.

Risking the truth is a game I will not play;
wrapped in August heat, I tell my father
it's summer; we know how she gets when it's hot.

Sailing through his eyes, I see a war rage;
he blinks, again; bombs explode behind his irises,
tears singe his cheeks. I step closer, hug him,

hold tight as he returns my embrace;
what else can I do through these August days
but pray peace will keep us a family.

August Eighth

Charles, I hold your name
safely on my tongue
slip it silently to my heart
      Pages in a family book whisper
      name, rank, serial number
      lengthy list of medals and citations
            8/8 Birth Certificate names
            your parents, Fannie and Matej
            Mike, the name on his mass card
                  Honorable Discharge papers
                  describe you blond, blue-eyed
                  Staff Sgt in '45; out in '46

A beige Certificate of Marriage
to Ethel, my mother-in-law
who rarely uttered your name
      Flip parchment pages that speak
      more to me of you
      than your blond, blue-eyed son
            Final page in your chapter
            yellow Death Certificate
            silent
                  Tell me; when I think of you
                  is it Charles, or Charlie
                  or Dad?

Aunt Mary and Uncle Mike

      My brother Mikey and I knew her
as the best-meatballs-and-gravy-ever aunt,
he was the uncle with a schnoz
like Jimmy Durante, though I doubt
he ever said *ahh-cha-cha-cha-cha-cha*.
      They had a house across the street
from my paternal grandparents
in Richmond Hill, Queens.
Aunt Mary and Uncle Mike
lived in the basement
or so we believed because we never
saw the upstairs of their house,
      except for the time I snuck up
the stairs tiptoeing all the way
to the museum white living room.
There must have been other furniture
but all I remember is the pristine couch
covered in plastic.
      I don't know if it was the sound
of the creaking basement door
or my bare thighs squelching across
the couch cover
that drew my mother upstairs,
silent index finger admonishment
to *get back down those stairs
this instant.*
      Next morning, I described
the austereness of the room
(though paraphrased as I was barely four)
Mikey was jealous; after all,
he was older, and the brave one.
      He pouted as we stood in front
of the open refrigerator door
eating baseball-big meatballs leftover
from dinner; he smiled when I hugged him,
rich red gravy dribbling from his chin
down my back.

Automation

No more push mowers to trim lawns
now exhaust fumes kill the grass,
the weeds, the earthworms.

No more turn on the tap and drink
now plastic bottles float beside ducks
swimming in a pond of debris.

No more corner phone booths
now cell phones ring out on streets
teeming with private-aired conversations.

No more paperbacks in back pockets
now books hide inside phones and tablets
that play music, ring music, and ping.

No more standing on long lines in stores
now online credit card buys are shipped
and soon returned via UPS all from home.

No more parks and preserves
now concrete and asphalt skim coat over
damaged landscapes.

No more snail mail letters
now emails and facebook and twitter
tells us how happy we should be.

Awakening

When sleep still slits our eyes
when dawn's just birthed the sky
if only we could peer into the day
beyond the cloaking veil of grey
see what's in store for the next 24.

Sunny bright ideas on verdant fields
skipping headlong into birdsong
or cloud cover threatening horizon-
wide smiles with doom
of gloomy forecast.

Something to spice up the mundane
awakening a palette of happenings
destined to determine dreams
the preceding night, if only
we were blessed with second sight.

Then on days that challenge us
beyond the road's edge,
days like today,
on awakening,
we could decide to stay in bed.

*****

    awkward
    meeting friends
    you met through friends
    you don't speak to anymore

(Senryu)

ACKNOWLEDGMENTS

"A Backyard Visit" *Imagistics*, Local Gems Press, 2015

"A Day in the Life" and "Augmentation"
Bards Annual 2011, Local Gems Press, 2011

"A Man-Plan" and "All Because of a Parking Space"
Grassroot Reflections, Volume 26, February 2013

"A Message from Mother Earth"
Grassroot Reflections, Volume 32, November 2014

"Across the Plains"
Friends of Hempstead Plains 2007 Anthology of Poetry

"Advancements" and "Automation"
Grassroot Reflections, Volume 35, May 2015

"All God's Children"   *The Sound of Poetry*, anthology 1992

"All My Friends Are Dead" *Bards Annual 2015*, Local Gems

"Alternatives"
Grassroot Reflections, Volume 25, November 2012

"An Untold Tale"
Long Island Sounds 2007, The North Sea Poetry Scene Press
and *Voice of the Bards*, Local Gems Poetry Press, 2011

"And She's Not Blonde"
Rhyme & PUN-ishment, Local Gems Press, 2012

"Art of the Bargain"
Grassroot Reflections, Volume 19, May 2011

"At the Death of Winter"
Paumanok: Poems and Pictures of Long Island
Cross Cultural Communications, 2009

"August Eighth" *They Come And They Go*, J R Turek
L I Expressions, 2005

ABOUT THE AUTHOR

J R (Judy) Turek, Bards Laureate 2013-2015, is 19 years as Moderator of the Farmingdale Creative Writing Group; recipient of 2 Pushcart nominations; and Nassau County, Suffolk County, NYS Assembly, and NYS Senate Proclamations for her lifetime dedication to poetry. She is co-editor of the poetry anthologies *Whispers and Shouts* and *Young Voices*, and author of the poetry collections *Imagistics* and *They Come And They Go*.

J R is an editor, internationally published poet, workshop leader, Board Member for The North Scene Poetry Scene (TNSPS), Princess Ronkonkoma Productions (PRP), Performance Poets Association (PPA); Editor and Council Member for The Bards Initiative, and poetry venue host for PPA. Her publications include over a hundred anthologies and periodicals.

She has been awarded poetry first place from The North Sea Poetry Scene, Mid Island Y JCC, Performance Poets Association Annual Poetry Contest and Haiku Contest, Princess Ronkonkoma Productions, noted placements from *Writer's Digest*, the Long Island Fair, Live Poets Society, Towe Auto Museum, and *Newsday's* Garden Poetry Contest; she is a recipient of the Conklin Prize For Poetry. She has performed her poetry at Walt Whitman Birthplace, Cedarmere - the home of poet William Cullen Bryant, Sagamore Hill, Tilles Center for the Performing Arts, and scores of libraries, coffee shops, and tattoo parlors across Long Island.

She is a poem-a-dayer for over 12 years. J R, the Purple Poet, lives on Long Island with her soul-mate husband, her dogs, and her extraordinarily extensive shoe collection. Contact her at msjevus@optonline.net.

Local Gems Poetry Press is a small Long Island based poetry press dedicated to spreading poetry through performance and the written word. Local Gems believes that poetry is the voice of the people, and as the sister organization of the Bards Initiative, believes that poetry can be used to make a difference.

www.localgemspoetrypress.com

Made in the USA
Middletown, DE
30 January 2017